Mental Health

Mental health and well-being are becoming incre
education, yet schools frequently find themselves lacking the tools, time and resources
to tackle the issues. Mental health support is often seen as an additional responsibility
of the school setting, rather than a core aspect of it. This practical, fully accessible book
provides straightforward guidance and low-budget strategies to help school settings
get mental health support right. With a focus on the well-being of both students and
staff, chapters focus on techniques to develop self-esteem, manage behaviour and
build positive relationships at all levels.

Key features include:

- low-cost and easy-to-implement strategies suitable for the busy classroom environment,
as well as whole school approaches
- downloadable activities and planning sheets based on cognitive behavioural therapy
techniques
- a focus on building strong foundations based on mental health basics

Refreshingly honest and conscious of the realities of the school environment, this
book is a crucial tool for anybody working within education.

Samantha Garner is an education consultant and trainer specialising in Special
Educational Needs (SEN) and mental health. She is an ex-SENCo (Special Educational
Needs Coordinator) and a qualified cognitive behavioural therapist and child and
adolescent counsellor who has written her own Cognitive Behavioural Therapy (CBT)
mental health programme used in schools worldwide. Lauded for her honesty and
humour, Sam travels nationally and internationally to train and speak at conferences.

Mental Health in Education

Building Good Foundations

Samantha Garner

Routledge
Taylor & Francis Group

LONDON AND NEW YORK

First published 2020
by Routledge
2 Park Square, Milton Park, Abingdon, Oxon OX14 4RN

and by Routledge
52 Vanderbilt Avenue, New York, NY 10017

Routledge is an imprint of the Taylor & Francis Group, an informa business

British Library Cataloguing-in-Publication Data
A catalogue record for this book is available from the British Library

Library of Congress Cataloging-in-Publication Data
A catalog record for this book has been requested

ISBN: 978-1-138-38632-7 (pbk)
ISBN: 978-0-429-42686-5 (ebk)

Typeset in Sabon
by Apex CoVantage, LLC

www.routledge.com/9781138386327

To my mum and dad, Monica and Paul,
who gave me the strongest foundations possible.

Contents

Acknowledgements

Thank you to my (current) husband Adam, who was so patient with my imposter syndrome and varying moods whilst writing this. He makes all my referencing as it should be and formatted the script. Thank you to the many fabulous education professionals I read and hear regularly who inspire me and reassure me. Thank you to Katrina Hulme-Cross at Speechmark for providing me with this opportunity. And finally, thank you to my family and friends for being you.

Introduction

Introduction

AKA Why on earth should I read this book?

Mental health is a much-discussed topic in education, and indeed everywhere. There are regular reports in the news about pupils and teachers suffering increasing mental health concerns. Support agencies are struggling to cope, for a variety of reasons, and education settings are feeling isolated in knowing how to help staff and pupils. Depression, anxiety, self-harm and eating disorders are some of the common mental health issues faced in education on a daily basis.

New buzzwords have arisen in education around mental health, such as 'resilience', and mindfulness is viewed as a popular 'fix'. We are looking for 'things' to blame the increase of problems on, such as social media and technology. Many people label pupils as 'snowflakes' and moan how they can't cope with life pressures. Parents are criticised for not parenting right. Teachers are criticised for not teaching correctly. Many of the initiatives we look at focus on changing the young person to improve their mental health. We're led to believe that if we 'fix' them, we will 'fix' the problem.

There are many factors contributing to the increase of mental health issues and there isn't one 'fix-all' solution. What we have to do in education is look at our accountability and also what can we do to support the mental health and well-being of our pupils. Supporting mental health isn't just about implementing lots of add-ons or interventions. Getting a school counsellor is not going to fix all the problems. Nor will mindfulness. It's about looking at the environment that pupils and staff are in five days a week.

A lot of people question how much teachers should be involved in mental health. I regularly read and hear that teachers aren't mental health experts and so shouldn't get involved when pupils are suffering. The key is that mental health underpins everything, including learning. Education isn't just about the learning; it's about preparing pupils for life, being supportive human beings and wanting the best for our pupils. There is a lot we can do to support mental health and well-being. Whilst we cannot change many causes of issues, pupils spend a long time in education and at the very least we have a responsibility to ensure we don't cause harm to the development of a child, or their mental health and well-being.

The purpose of this book is to look at what we do environmentally to support good positive mental health and well-being and ensure we don't cause mental harm – for both staff and pupils.

I have highlighted eight areas to think about, hence the eight chapters in this book. These are the basic foundations for supporting positive mental health and well-being. If we get the basics right there will be less need for interventions, and the interventions we do use will be more effective. I spoke once to a psychiatrist who works in a young offenders institute. She was expected to 'rehabilitate' inmates with one-hour-a-week sessions. The rest of the time they were in a highly toxic environment, only feeling safe when locked in their room. She actually had to be careful not to leave the offender psychologically vulnerable and unable to cope back in the toxic environment. Although to a lesser extent, this is same in education. Having a counsellor will not fix mental health issues if the environment they return to is toxic and unsupportive. A counsellor alone is not enough. We have to get the basics and the environment right.

It's important that we don't become obsessed with 'fixing' when talking about mental health. We don't fix mental health issues. We support mental health and provide strategies to help manage life. I suffer with depression; it's never 'fixed', but I manage it (chocolate is heavily involved) and life is pretty good most of the time. The view of 'fixing' is similar to that I experienced as a SENCo. "Here's the child, fix them and send them back to me". It doesn't work like that.

This book is not intended as a dictatorial bible. You don't have to agree with me, and I respect your right to have a different opinion. It's designed to stimulate thought about your setting. It provides some suggestions with a few cognitive behavioural therapy tools to start you on the process.

There isn't one off-the-shelf mental health system or intervention that works for all. Supporting mental health and well-being is a system made up of many elements. What you have to embrace is the willingness to read and hear what is being said, to look critically at your setting and how you can improve. As the great Maya Angelou said, "Do the best you can until you know better. Then when you know better, do better".[1]

Ironically, by improving mental health and well-being, you will improve results. Deci, in his book *Self-Determination Theory*,[2] found from many studies that "when learning conditions are supportive of students' basic psychological needs, intrinsic motivation, well-being, and high-quality learning are likely to result". So, if this is all a bit 'touchy-feely' for you, just think of it in terms of improving results -- the ultimate aim of education at the moment (first controversial statement of the book).

This book also uses a lot of ideas from cognitive behavioural therapy (CBT). This is one of the most evidenced forms of therapy and underpins many other types of therapy. I love it so much I have trained as a therapist in it! So, what actually is CBT?

Very simply, CBT functions on the belief that we have a thought, which leads to a feeling, which leads to a behaviour. The behaviour has a consequence which usually reinforces our initial thought. It also theorises that our initial thoughts are based on our perceptions and experiences and can be changed. If we change the way we think, then we can change the ensuing behaviours and consequences. For example, you are walking down the street and you wave at someone. They don't wave back. This is even more embarrassing if you've shouted "Yoo-hoo" as well. If your initial thought is negative, such as "I've done something wrong and they don't like me any more", your feeling will be rejection and shame. Your behaviour next time you see them will be to avoid them, and the consequence is likely that you will not speak again: a negative outcome. If your initial thought is positive, such as "Ooh, I hope they're OK, because that's unusual for them to ignore me". Your feeling is concern, your behaviour is to ask them what's wrong next time you see them, and they will then explain what happened or apologise for not seeing you: a positive outcome. And that's CBT: changing our thoughts, our negative cognitive bias. It's not instant; it requires practice, but it does work.

OK, this is very simplistic, but the point is that nothing is fact; all that matters is our interpretation/perception which can be positive or negative. Our interpretations/perceptions can be changed. An underlying factor of many mental health issues is ruminative negative thinking. So, if we can change our thoughts to more positive/realistic ones and manage the negative ones, we will have better mental well-being.

The CBT activities here are worksheets for pupils to complete or conversation templates for staff to use. They are to facilitate new constructive conversations. They aren't a magic pill where you do it once and it's sorted. CBT only works if activities are practised and repeated. Adapt the language according the age and ability of your pupil. CBT ideas and language patterns are ideal for use in education. They can become embedded in day-to-day practise.

What are mental health and well-being? For me the terms are interchangeable, and this book isn't about deciding specific definitions of either. The World Health Organization describes them thus:

> Mental health is defined as a state of well-being in which every individual realizes his or her own potential, can cope with the normal stresses of life, can work productively and fruitfully, and is able to make a contribution to her or his community.[3]

I quite like that description. For me, good mental health and well-being is the ability to be able to cope with the bad parts of life and enjoy the good parts. It's not about being happy all the time. It's about knowing yourself, looking after yourself and liking yourself. Many people mistake positive thinking for being happy all the time and nothing being able to bother you. That's not it. It isn't about running through a field of poppies eating chocolate believing you will be happy for ever. It's about saying I will be OK. This is temporary, and I can deal with this. It's a bit pants at the moment, but I will get through it and I will be OK.

However, it's all about forward thinking, becoming proactive and not reactive. A perfect example is the Upstream parable. .

In the village of Downstream it was noticed that people kept floating down the river needing help. The villagers jumped in and rescued them. More people kept coming, so they bought a lifeboat. Then they built a rescue centre hospital on the side of the road at a cost of £1,000,000. They trained all their staff and congratulated themselves on a system that had a 50% success rate. Then somebody asked where the people were coming from; what was causing it? They took a walk up the river, and they found a village called Upstream (original I know). This village was on a cliff overlooking the river. People were looking over the cliff to see what was down there and then slipped and fell in. So, the Downstream villagers spent £200 putting a fence on the cliff to stop people falling in and greatly reduced the need for the expensive facilities in their village. Ta-da!

OK, it may not that simple and I may have embellished the parable a little (writer's license), but we all know early intervention works. And prevention works even better. We are a long way off achieving zero mental health issues. However, we can counteract some of the causes, and by making sure our foundations are good, we can go a long way towards early intervention and prevention. We can also ensure the scarce resources can be focused on those pupils who need it. Having good mental health and well-being amongst staff should reduce staff sick days.[4]

Paying for expensive interventions without ensuring the basics are right is like having a very expensive car then putting cheap tyres on it so it can't be driven correctly. There are lots of analogies that I could use, but I hope you get the picture. It's about building good foundations (sounds like a good title for a book).

At the end of each chapter are activities and supporting resources related to that chapter. Chapter 9 is an audit you may want to use for your setting.

This isn't a psychological scientific manual. There are lots of those about. This is a straight-talking book to help staff and pupils. I try not to use elitist language to sound intelligent – you won't need a dictionary to read this. I use the words *pupil* and *setting*. This isn't intended to alienate anyone; they can be substituted for *student, child, young person, school, college,* etc. Let's agree that a 'pupil' is 4–21 years old and a 'setting' is an educational establishment. I also try to use humour and no doubt some of it you won't find funny. That's OK, it makes me smile. I do joke about PE teachers, as that's my 'thing', and I am *not* a sports person. I do need to point out some of my closest friends are PE teachers (yeah, that old chestnut). One ex-PE teacher friend asked if PE teachers get mentioned, and I said "Of course, but most PE teachers don't read books, so I am safe". He said "Well, if they do, they will move their lips whilst reading". Straight from the horse's mouth!

Happy reading.

References

1   Dr Angelou, M (2018). *Do the Best You Can Until You Know Better: Then When You Know Better, Do Better* [Tweet]. Available from: https://twitter.com/DrMayaAngelou?lang=en

2   Ryan, R.M & Deci, E.L (2018). *Self-Determination Theory*. New York: The Guildford Press.

3   Who.int (2019). *World Health Organisation*. [Online]. [2 May 2019]. Available from: www.who.int/features/factfiles/mental_health/en/

4   Milligan-Saville, JS et al (2017). *Workplace Mental Health Training for Managers and Its Effect on Sick Leave in Employees: A Cluster Randomised Controlled Trial*. England: The Lancet Psychiatry. November (Volume 4, Issue 11, pp 850–8). [3 May 2019]. Available from: www.sciencedirect.com/science/article/pii/S2215036617303723?fbclid=IwA R1PYwfn85A4ETD-A1zGHuj01Wc5b6WKoM01zgXBUbguu_dlphYcDSa9rj0

Chapter 1

Staff mental health and well-being

Look after the biggest resource

AKA We have to look after staff first!

When we talk about mental health and well-being in education, we are mainly referring to pupils. But what about staff? Staff are the biggest resource in education, and they must be a priority. Staff mental health and well-being is crucial. We cannot talk about mental health in education without discussing staff mental health and well-being, for two reasons. Firstly, staff are human beings (even some of the PE teachers) and their mental health is important, for their own life and for staff retention. Secondly, their mental health, and emotional literacy, is one of the biggest, if not the biggest, influence on pupil mental health and well-being in an education setting.

Staff mental health issues have increased and we are losing a high number of teaching days because of it. In a survey conducted by Leeds Becket University, over half the respondents had a diagnosed mental health condition and the vast majority of respondents believed their mental health issues had a negative effect in the classroom.[1] For those of us who work in mental health, this isn't a surprise. We understand that mental well-being underpins and affects everything. Everything. Once more for emphasis: EVERYTHING!

Think back to your life up to the age of 16. Who were the key influential people, positive and/or negative, in your life? Now think of the negative influences. I expect they have left you with some lasting negative thoughts about yourself. Think about the mental health of those key influential people. Did they have good positive mental health? Were they emotionally literate (understanding and empathetic)? In most cases I suggest not. For most of you there will be a teacher and/or fellow pupil on either of your lists. Perhaps some are on both the positive and negative list, as this is also possible. You will still remember how they made you feel, and any negative influences can leave deep emotional scars. This is the same for pupils today and we have to ensure that we are a positive, not negative, influence.

As mentioned in the introduction, this isn't just about being touchy-feely with snowflakes. Supporting pupil mental health and well-being will improve results. The relationship between teacher and pupil is one of the key elements in effective pupil learning. This is supported by lots of research, including:

- "What makes great pedagogy? Nine claims from research"[2]
- John Hattie, "Invisible Learning"[3] and
- *Improving Pupils' Relationships with Teachers to Provide Essential Supports for Learning*[4]

Building good relationships and having good emotional literacy is great pedagogy. It's part of being a teacher, of working in education. In order to do this, we have to have good mental health ourselves.

Building positive relationships

AKA Being nice to people

Building positive relationships is the basis for everything in life: in business, in personal relationships, everything. It is one of the key elements of happiness according to self-determination theory. Not having positive relationships is a factor in many mental health issues. Our own mental well-being affects our ability to build positive relationships with others (including pupils). It's vital we acknowledge this.

I suffer with depression, which many people are surprised at because I 'don't seem that sort', which I always think is a tactful way of saying I'm gobby. I manage my depression with medication, understanding, chocolate and CBT techniques. My mental health still has 'troughs', but I can recognise the signs. Symptoms of a down period: I reduce my social interaction, sleep more, am angrier and have less capacity to manage stress. It also affects my relationships – the effort of being nice is really hard when so often I just want to say "Fluff off" (you know what I really mean), and retreat to bed to eat chocolate (are you seeing a theme here?). I will try to sabotage relationships and not make effort, when relationships are exactly what I need to help me out of the trough.

When in a trough, my capacity for empathy, and therefore, a positive response to a situation, is affected. It is either reduced or I am completely exhausted by the effort of maintaining 'the nice mask'. When in a 'down' phase, it's really hard to give two hoots about other people's problems. Understanding and discussing this is important – it means I can take steps to improve my mental health and prevent the severity of the depression. Not just better for me, but also for those around me.

Good mental health means we are more able to manage stress. Lazarus and Folkman have developed a transactional model of stress.[5] They believe stress occurs when there is an imbalance between demand and resource. When demand exceeds resource we become stressed. But, they discovered that our interpretation is more important than actual facts. How we subjectively assess the stressful event or situation, and our abilities for coping with it are of more importance. This ties in with CBT beliefs – that everything is our interpretation. Stress is about our perception of the demand, our ability to cope, and what the consequences of being unable to meet the demand will be. We can get stuck in ruminative negative thinking – another common factor in mental health issues. If we have positive mental health and well-being, we are less likely to have negative thoughts about our capacity to meet demand, and the negative consequences if we don't meet demand.

Stress is also important because when we are very stressed, we are more likely to personalise people's behaviour towards us. We are more likely to believe someone is doing something on purpose to annoy us. When we are late, we become angrier at traffic jams and are likely to gesticulate or swear at someone (a daily occurrence for some). The most annoying pupil will always be more annoying when we are tired, and we can think they are surely doing it on purpose to 'wind us up'. Believing a person is doing something on purpose will affect our reaction to it. Dagnan, Hull and McDonnell identified the controllability beliefs scale[6] where judgements of responsibility predict our emotional response to an action. If we believe a person is doing an action on purpose, we are less likely to have a sympathetic response. Having a less sympathetic response means a situation is more likely to escalate in a negative way. If we believe the person isn't doing it purposely, that it's part of their condition or they are communicating something to us, we are more likely to have a sympathetic response and a more positive outcome.

By being more stressed, and personalising others' behaviour, we are more likely to have a confrontational response to a situation. This will, in many situations, escalate to a negative outcome that could have been avoided. We've all had those conversations where we escalate up and up and end up with nowhere to go. "Well, if you are late again you will end up being expelled from every setting in the whole world, for ever". I do it with my children: "If you don't clear that up then this will happen". They argue back, and I get angrier and escalate the consequences to impossible scenarios: "You are grounded for 35 years and I am taking everything out of your bedroom". I then walk away thinking "How the hell am I going to follow through on that? I wish I handled that differently". A sympathetic response is less likely to escalate and more likely to have a more positive outcome.

Modelling

AKA The "Do as I say, not as I do" mentality doesn't work

Our biggest influence on pupils is what and who we are – that is, through modelling. Our mental health and well-being is important to that modelling. We have to understand and openly discuss mental health and well-being to model that to pupils to reduce stigma. I had a conversation once with my daughters about why they only see the negative things about themselves when looking in a mirror. They said "You do too, Mum". And they were right – which obviously I hated them for, as no one wants their children to be right! But it made me realise how important modelling is. They had learned many of their behaviours from me. So now I remark how fabulous I look when I look in a mirror (and I do, obviously).

When training I often ask staff "Are you nice to each other? Are you nice to all your pupils? Do you have a competitive environment amongst staff?" This competitive toxic environment will be modelled by the pupils. A Hughes, Calle and Wilson (2001)[7] study showed that classmates make inferences on other attributes and likeability based in part on observations of teacher interactions. Gest and Rodkin[8] showed that teachers who showed a high level of emotional support to all pupils had classrooms with more reciprocated friendships. We are going to see later how important friendships are to mental health, but here's a clue – IT'S MASSIVE.

If we have positive mental health and well-being, we are more likely to be nicer to pupils who in turn will be nicer to each other.

Our influence and impact via modelling are further verified in a meta-analysis by Sanchez, Cornacchio et al.[9] They found that "[c]onsidering serious barriers precluding youth from accessing necessary mental health care, . . . child psychiatrists and other mental health professionals are wise to recognize the important role that school personnel, who are naturally in children's lives, can play in decreasing child mental health problems".

Are you a positive model or a negative model for your pupils? Are you emotionally regulated? Do you demonstrate effective self-regulation of your emotions?

Being an emotionally regulated role model is vital in supporting mental health. Hauser, Allen & Golden (2006)[10] found that teenagers who had committed violent crimes and developed insight and self-awareness, went on to do well, and that a major part of this had to do with capacities developed through talking with adults who modelled psychological thinking. Now, I am not saying we should start working with deeply traumatised and violent teenagers, but that by being good self-regulated role models we have a major influence on the mental health and well-being of our pupils. Teachers who regularly lose their temper and shout are not modelling self-regulated behaviour – this will be discussed further in a later chapter.

Emotional literacy

AKA Understanding how and why we don't all think the same

Part of having good mental health and well-being ourselves is about having good emotional literacy. By this I mean a good understanding of how we think and how other people think, why people may feel as they do, what can affect this and how it can be supported, how we work and how pupils work. Most importantly, we must understand we are all different with different perceptions and different emotions. It's important that we know enough never to say "Well, I went through worse and I was OK, so get on with it".

So often I hear that mental health training isn't a priority, or mental health training for staff is optional, not compulsory. "We only have a certain amount of Continuing Professional Development (CPD) time, and we have higher priorities". This is very short-sighted, as mental well-being underpins *everything* (everything). Mental health and well-being aren't just about results; however, in an education world currently obsessed with results, I often bring it down to that outcome to try and persuade people to 'buy in'. It will probably be more effective than any other CPD training on the latest 'thing' (apart from differentiation, as that's really important).

In order to connect with others and build positive relationships, we must understand how the brain develops and the impact of early development on the amygdala and hippocampus and how this controls how we behave. It is vital that staff receive regular training on the basics of brain development and mental health, the impact of trauma and adverse childhood experiences (ACES), how to support pupils and how to support their own mental health and well-being.

How to listen properly

AKA Don't tell me you had it worse

At the very least, staff should know how to listen, and hear, to listen and hear pupils and each other. On the simplest level, just listening and hearing a child is one of the best things you can do for mental health and well-being. Being listened to is also good for our own mental health and well-being.

Listening properly means we hear what pupils are saying and acknowledge how they are feeling. We don't dismiss them, tell them they are being silly, or that they have nothing to worry about. We don't say "You have nothing to worry about", or "Other people have it worse", or "It's your own fault".

We like to try to make people feel better by telling them how much worse it could have been. That they should look on the bright side and acknowledge the good things. Yes, it's true it could have been worse, but that isn't acknowledging the immediate feeling of distress. "Ooh, you were lucky in that car crash". Um, what part of a car crash is lucky? We are uncomfortable when people cry and as a result we try to ensure we don't say anything to make them cry. So, we make a "stiff upper lip, get on with it" comment.

I had a horse-riding accident some years ago. I was airlifted off Dartmoor and broke my pelvis and shoulder. I was in hospital for a while with tubes and metal pins, and all I could move for a while was one arm. People would visit and the first thing they would say was "Blimey, you're lucky, it could have been so much worse". Really? F*** off (I was in a lot of pain). If I were lucky, I would still be on the horse. Instead I am here in pain and it would be nice if you could acknowledge that. And you could also have bought chocolate because I can eat that with one hand. I made it for three days with a stiff upper lip before crying my eyes out with built-up, unacknowledged emotion and pain.

It's OK to just say "That sounds so hard, thank you for sharing. How can I help?" That's it. When I am going through a difficulty, I don't want to know you had it worse, or that at least my hair looks nice, or that it's nothing to worry about. I want someone to hear me and acknowledge it. It won't make it worse; it will make me feel better that I have been heard and that I shared it. Think about it. When you are stressed you will avoid people who will tell you it's all your own fault and that if you had listened to them it would be all be okay. Don't be that person for other people. Be someone who listens and hears; the person who acknowledges what they are going through and that's it's pants. If you've seen *Inside Out* ©2015 Walt Disney Pictures, there is a scene where the elephant is upset. Joy tries to make him feel better with distraction and cheery things. Sadness listens and acknowledges his pain (*this is what makes him feel better*).

This is the most important skill for all staff to learn. In education we have a fear that we are going to make things worse if we say the wrong thing, or we feel we must have expert skills to support pupil mental health. You don't. You have to listen, hear and acknowledge. These are immensely powerful skills. Remember, we never 'fix' children, we aim to make their lives better and the first step in doing this is listening, hearing and acknowledging. Just having one person who hears us and believes us can make a major difference – adults and children.

Listening works:

- "Children who are empathised with on a regular basis in childhood have a good vagal tone (calm body states), and do better academically, socially and emotionally".[11]
- "When people are in pain, an empathetic presence calms the body".[12]

Open staff culture

AKA Staff mental health and well-being should an open topic for discussion without fear of reprisals

Is there a culture of being able to talk about mental health in your setting? This is where I personally think education has some way to go – that we need to be able to have open discussion without repercussion. I have always been open about my mental health, but this has been used against me when I was employed (before I began to work for myself as I do now) and it was horrible. I hear many stories about it being done to staff and it is not acceptable. It is indicative of poor management skills. When I hear some speakers say to be open about mental health in your setting, I do advise that you do it with caution and depending on the setting and management. Only do it if there is a supportive element amongst staff with regard to mental health. Mental health and well-being should not be a stick to beat staff with.

The importance of humour

AKA A regular good laugh is good medicine

Did you know that when you smile, even if it's forced, it produces happy chemicals? It's an automatic reflex thingamabob (technical term). Humour is one of the great techniques for managing stress and is important for good mental well-being. We must have fun in our life. So, ask yourself, do you laugh enough? Is there fun in your workplace? Is there fun at home? If not, what makes you laugh? Do it more often. If not, what can you do to laugh more? What can you put in place to bring more fun to work? I could make suggestions, but my sense of humour may not be to everyone's taste (if you ever see me, do ask me about the story of Mum getting in the wrong car outside Walmart in Florida – hilarious!)

Humour is one of the best techniques for relieving stress. When I came home after my accident and subsequent operation, I was a bit down, as I thought my broken shoulder and pelvis would miraculously be fixed once home. Surprise, surprise; they weren't. My dad then gave me all the car parking receipts from visiting me at hospital and said I could refund him when ready. We laughed. A lot. And I felt better.

Ask staff for ideas! Fun increases productivity in addition to promoting good mental well-being!

Remember how valued you are

AKA You are a fabulous person making a difference

Part of staff mental well-being is being reminded on a regular basis how fabulous you are. What a difference you are making to the lives of pupils. How you are shaping the future of our planet. How lucky you are to be in that position. Pupils will look back and remember you with fondness and how you made a difference to their life. Now that I work for myself I miss being able to build positive relationships with pupils working with them on a regular basis. Yes, pupils can be a pain, other staff can be immensely irritating, parents can be a nightmare and unnecessary paperwork builds up and up. However, despite all the crap, it can be a great job and you are very special. Make sure you are reminded of this on a regular basis.

Techniques to support staff mental well-being

AKA Come on then, Garner, enough blah blah, what do I do?

I'm not one for saying this is how you must do it. This is a list of suggestions that may or may not work for you and your setting. They are just a starting point for you to think about, discuss and implement if you like them (AKA they are brilliant suggestions, but I like to appear modest now and then).

Staff survey

The very first action is to see where you are now with regard to staff mental well-being and emotional literacy. A suggested questionnaire is at the end of this chapter. What is crucial is that the survey is anonymous. If you want the truth, it has to be anonymous. I visited one setting where the staff were asked to complete a survey. They weren't told the overall results of the survey and some staff were called in to be asked why they had said certain negative things on the survey! The setting did not ask staff to complete a survey again. This is not using a survey properly. If you want to improve, you have to know where you are now. And know honestly. Staff are mostly adult enough to refrain from writing obscenities or drawing penises everywhere (can't guarantee with PE teachers though), but if you want true opinion it must be anonymous. It also must be regular to evaluate progress and update action plans.

Staff mental well-being team

Set up a staff mental well-being team who have the remit of promoting and supporting staff mental well-being. Have a link to Senior Leadership Team (SLT) – this may be a member of the SLT, but this can sometimes be restrictive as people will not be able to be candid. Pick the 'right' SLT person or instead make sure you have a connection to SLT somehow.

Ask for volunteers but also encourage the less likely staff – the ones with the more 'well-established mindsets'. You need a range of staff opinions and representatives as the team is for all staff. You may even wish to have a PE teacher on the team.

Outline how often they will meet, when, where, etc., and what their objectives are. Use the anonymous survey results as a starting point.

Set up staff activities

There are lots of activities that can be set up without high cost. Do you have a yoga expert who could run staff yoga sessions? What about a staff football team or similar sporty stuff like that for strange people who like that sort of thing? A staff choir – music is fabulous therapy! Ask for suggestions and staff to run activities.

Encourage work-life balance

Close your setting at 4.00pm or 5.00pm at least one day a week to ensure staff go home on time. Perhaps shut down the email system between the hours of 8.00pm and 7.00am and on Sundays. Staff can access and draft emails, but no emails can be sent or received. Your IT department may deny it can be done (you know what IT people are like), but apparently it is possible.

Duvet days

This one will be a little harder to achieve cost-wise but worth thinking about. I know a setting that allows each member of staff one day a term to have off to do something for themselves; for example, a mental health or duvet day. This seems expensive – but think of the staff sickness bill. Would some preventative action be saving costs down the line? Whilst I have no empirical evidence that it would yet, as it is a new concept, from personal experience I believe it would save money long-term.

Encourage social interaction

Social isolation is one of the common factors in many mental health issues. Could you encourage more social interaction? Perhaps mix up groups in CPD sessions, do a secret Santa scheme not just at Christmas. Ask staff to work with each other to set up activities previously mentioned. We all feel better after positive social interaction, laughing and smiling. Being in education can be quite isolating, so we have to be aware of this especially in independent settings where the majority of staff live on site. It can be a 'bubble' experience.

Access to a counsellor or mental health support

Are staff able to access mental health support easily and confidentially? Are they given time to access this support during work hours? Early access to support and an easily accessible system will reap benefits.

Using a personal positive model

We will often work on a deficit model of our achievements. That is, we will focus on what we haven't done – what we need to do rather that what we have done. This is a common negative thought trap identified in CBT: only seeing the negative or discounting any positives by pointing out what hasn't been done. Ruminative negative thinking is a common factor in many mental health issues, so changing this mindset is important to positive mental well-being. There are some simple CBT activities at the end of this chapter that can help you to recognise positive achievements and change your cognitive bias.

Support managing stress

There should be open discussions about stress and about how to manage it. Discuss how stress can be supported in your setting and how you can affect perceptions of stress to support mental well-being. Again, there are some simple CBT activities at the end of this chapter to help staff manage stress. SLT also have to look at what part they play in contributing to staff stress. I know there are limits because the 'system' is causing stress, but there are things SLT can do to reduce this for themselves and staff.

Have a nice staffroom

Is the staffroom a nice place to relax? Is it nicely decorated? Is there cake/chocolate freely available? Are there colouring-in books and pencils? Lego/play dough to play with? These are all relaxing activities. Have a whiteboard where staff can write nice things that happened. Make sure the staffroom is a 'no-bollocking' room as this will change the mentality of staff about the staffroom. Just as pupils need a safe place, so do staff.

N.B. Don't allow the staff noticeboard for comments to be misused. I heard of a staff member that complimented everyone in the setting office except for one person they didn't like. This is intimidating behaviour and not acceptable. If the board is misused, remove it or speak to staff about inappropriate use.

Chapter summary

- Staff are the biggest resource.
- Staff mental well-being and emotional literacy should be a priority.

- We must build positive relationships with pupils.
- What we model has a major impact on pupils.
- Staff need regular compulsory mental health training.
- We must have good emotional literacy and understanding.
- Listening to and acknowledging pupils is vital.
- Staff mental health must be discussed and supported.
- Encourage fun.
- Remember how fabulous and valued you are.

Supporting tools and activities

STAFF SURVEY

Possible questions you may wish to ask your staff regarding their mental well-being. Surveys can be simply done using online tools. Or by using old-fashioned paper!

Staff mental health

- Do you feel there is a supportive atmosphere amongst staff in our setting?
- Do you feel the SLT are supportive of staff mental well-being?
- Do you know where to go if you need further support for your mental health?
- Do you feel you are achieving a suitable work-life balance?
- Which areas of your job cause you the most stress? For example, colleagues, SLT, pupils, results, expectations, workload, inspections, external pressures such as family commitments, parents, finances?
- Which areas of your job do you enjoy the most?
- Do you currently have a mental health concern?
- If yes, are you receiving support for that mental health concern?
- Is there anything we can put in place to support your mental health concern?
- Do you feel able to manage the stresses of the job in the long-term?
- Do you feel able to discuss your mental health freely in the setting without repercussion?
- What do you feel the setting does well with regard to supporting staff mental well-being?
- What do you feel the setting could improve to support staff mental well-being?
- Do you have any suggestions of what could be put in place to support staff mental well-being?

Pupil mental health

- Do you feel comfortable discussing mental health and well-being with pupils?
- Do you know what to say to a pupil experiencing obvious distress?
- Do you know where to refer a pupil who needs mental health support?
- Do you feel the setting addresses bullying effectively?
- What training have you received around mental health and well-being?
- What areas of training around mental health would you like in the future?
- What do you feel we could do to improve support we provide for pupil mental health and well-being?

Managing stress – CBT-based activity

Changing how we think about stress can reduce its impact on our mental wellbeing. Complete this chart regularly until it becomes a habitual way of thinking, then use as needed.

What is causing me stress at the moment?	
What can I currently change or control?	
What do I worry will happen if I cannot manage the stress?	
How likely is it to happen? Has this happened before?	
What will I do if it does come true?	
What would I advise a friend to do in this situation?	
Is there an alternative way I could think about this/is my fear rational? What could I tell myself?	

Managing stress – CBT-based activity – Example worksheet

Changing how we think about stress can reduce its impact on our mental wellbeing. Complete this chart regularly until it becomes a habitual way of thinking, then use as needed.

Question	Response
What is causing me stress at the moment?	My workload, the amount of writing and paperwork I have to do
What can I currently change or control?	How I think about my workload How I schedule my workload
What do I worry will happen if I cannot manage the stress?	I will appear unprofessional I will let people down I will lose work
How likely is it to happen? Has this happened before?	It has happened once or twice but the majority of times I have managed. I haven't lost work
What will I do if it does come true?	I will apologise and look to how I can address the problem I will look at how much work I can accept in the future
What would I advise a friend to do in this situation?	To do their best To schedule and prioritise To explain to manager the concerns about managing workload
Is there an alternative way I could think about this/is my fear rational? What could I tell myself?	I have usually been able to manage workload and when I couldn't it was okay. I will prioritise and do what I can, I will be okay whatever happens

Recognising how great you are!

Tasks I completed this week	Nice things that happened to me this week	Things that made me laugh this week	What I did for myself this week	What will I do for myself next week? (Give details)

Recognising how great you are! – Example worksheet

Tasks I completed this week	Nice things that happened to me this week	Things that made me laugh this week	What I did for myself this week	What will I do for myself next week? (Give details)
Completed data analysis.	Pupil thanked me for help	Cat videos on Facebook	3 baths	Tuesday - Swimming
Caught up on marking.	Parent said child enjoyed my class	Pupil response to a question	Swimming	Sunday - go for a walk
Planned next week	At chocolate	Men falling over a bench	Lie-in Sunday	Friday - go home at 3:30pm
Ironing!	Ate out Friday evening	Joke in the staffroom		Get my hair done
Food shopping		Comedy show on TV		

Area	Benefit	What do you do?
Work	Creativity Stumulation Interaction Productivity Financial	
Social	Friends, recreational activities, interaction with other groups of people	
Healthy Lifestyle	Regular sleep patterns, sensible eating, healthy body, exercise/activity	
Relaxation	Personal space, downtime, time away from work/social media/chores etc.	
Family	Love, procreation, belonging to a group, support, identity	
Hobbies	Productivity, social interaction, creative, stimulation	

Life balance – CBT activity

Area	Benefit	What do you do?
Work	Creativity Stumulation Interaction Productivity Financial	*Teaching* *Singing* *Exam paper marking*
Social	Friends, recreational activities, interaction with other groups of people	*Singing* *Watch cricket or rugby* *Meals with friends*
Healthy Lifestyle	Regular sleep patterns, sensible eating, healthy body, exercise/activity	*Swimming* *Active lifestyle* *Dancing*
Relaxation	Personal space, downtime, time away from work/social media/chores etc.	*Baths* *Swimming* *Singing*
Family	Love, procreation, belonging to a group, support, identity	*Close family* *Rugby* *Friends*
Hobbies	Productivity, social interaction, creative, stimulation	*Knitting* *Reading fiction novels* *I don't do enough!*

References

1   Glazzard, J (2018). *Pupil Progress Held Back by Teachers' Poor Mental Health*. [Online]. England: Leeds Beckett University and teachwire.net. [26 April 2019]. Available from: www.leedsbeckett.ac.uk/news/0118-mental-health-survey/ Results www.teachwire.net/news/pupil-progress-is-being-held-back-by-teachers-poor-mental-health

2   Husbands, C & Pearce, J (2012). *What makes great pedagogy? Nine claims from research*. [Online]. England: National College for School Leadership. [26 April 2019]. Available from: https://assets.publishing.service.gov.uk/government/uploads/system/uploads/attachment_data/file/329746/what-makes-great-pedagogy-nine-claims-from-research.pdf

3   Hattie, J (2008). *Visible Learning*. New York: Routledge.

4   Rimm-Kaufman, S & Sandilos, L (n.d.). *Improving Students' Relationships with Teachers to Provide Essential Supports for Learning*. [Online]. VA: University of Virginia. [26 April 2019]. Available from: www.apa.org/education/k12/relationships

5   Lazarus, R.S & Folkman, S (c1987). *Transactional Theory and Research on Emotions and Coping*. Chichester: John Wiley & Sons, Ltd.

6   Dagnan, D et al (2013). The controllability beliefs scale used with carers of people with intellectual disabilities: psychometric properties. *Journal of Intellectual Disability Research: JIDR*. 57, 5: 422–8.

7   Hughes, J.N, Cavell, T.A & Willson, V (2001). Further Support for the Developmental Significance of the Quality of the Teacher – Student Relationship. *Texas A&M University: Journal of School Psychology*. 39, 4.

8   Gest, S & Rodkin, P (2011). Teaching Practices and Elementary Classroom Peer Ecologies. *Journal of Applied Developmental Psychology*. 32: 288–96. doi: 10.1016/j.appdev.2011.02.004

9   Sanchez, L.A, Cornacchio, D, Chou, T, Leyfer, O, Coxe, S, Pincus, D & Comer, J (2016). Development of a Scale to Evaluate Young Children's Responses to Uncertainty and Low Environmental Structure. *Journal of Anxiety Disorders*. 45. doi: 10.1016/j.janxdis.2016.11.006

10   Hauser, S.T, Allen, J.P & Golden, E (2006). *Adolescent Lives 4: Out of the Woods: Tales of Resilient Teens*. Cambridge, MA: Harvard University Press.

11   Gladstone, G.L, Parker, G.B & Malhi, G.S (2006). *The Journal of Nervous and Mental Disease* (Volume 4, Issue 3, pp 201–8 ed.). New York: Wolters Kluwer.

12   Sambo, C, Howard, M, Kopelman, M, Williams, S & Fotopoulou, A (2010). Knowing You Care: Effects of Perceived Empathy and Attachment Style on Pain Perception. *Pain*. 151: 687–93. doi: 10.1016/j.pain.2010.08.035

Chapter 2

Self-esteem

Why self-esteem is important

AKA Self-esteem is really, really, really important!

How's your self-esteem? Is it good? Is it bad? If I were to ask you three things you like about yourself, and three things you don't, which three would be easier to come up with? For the majority of us it's easier to come up with three negative things about ourselves – and probably more! I bet the majority of these negative beliefs stem from your childhood. From your experiences at home and/or at school. I speak to mature (AKA old) adults who have been successful in their career, but they believe aren't clever because they failed the 11+ exam. That stigma has stayed with them for all those years and affected their self-esteem. They believe they are stupid.

Low self-esteem is one of the most common, if not the most common, factor in the majority of mental health issues. Good self-esteem is important for resilience and yet it seems the education system works against good self-esteem and resilience for staff and pupils.

Let's talk about resilience

AKA I blooming hate how 'resilience' has been hijacked by education as the 'go-to' thing

I am often asked how to improve the resilience of pupils. We believe that if children had more resilience everything would be great, and all mental health problems would disappear. I'm not a fan of the word *resilience*, particularly how it's manipulated for use in education. When education (as a thing – I did say you wouldn't need a dictionary) talks about resilience it really means we want you to be able to cope with an education system that focuses on what you can't do and that may not be suitable for your needs, but tough. We want you to be able to cope with us telling you that you're not good enough and have to work harder.

Also, resilience isn't just about what is in you. A major part of resilience is about who is around you, your support network. I am quite a strong resilient person and one of the key reasons for that is I have a fabulous support network of people around me. I didn't get through my hard times alone; the people around me made it so much easier. Many children and families don't have large support networks, which lowers resilience. Poverty lowers resilience. When we had snow recently my train got stuck on frozen points about 10 miles from my home. My dad had a 4x4 and came to pick me up. He also transported other people who didn't have someone with a 4x4. These little things contribute to resilience. An ex-pupil contacted me once to ask if I had an old mobile phone he could borrow as his had broken and he needed one for his job. He wasn't being paid until the end of the month. He had been through the care system and as an adult didn't have a wide support network. I had a drawer full of old phones, so it was not a problem. All these things add up to our resilience, so don't ever think it's just about what is within the person.

I find the implication that children who do not take criticism well have low resilience to be offensive and ignorant. Having worked with young people in many environments, I've seen incredible resilience – much more than I will ever have – on a daily basis. Getting up each day and keeping going when their whole life is traumatic and disruptive is major resilience – more than many people who complain about 'snowflakes' have. To say they're not resilient because they get 'upset' being told they're stupid, is patronising and misinformed.

Resilience is also fluid, it's not a constant. On a daily basis my resilience is a lot lower late at night when I am tired. No one in my family speaks to me if I get tired. It's dangerous, quite frankly; think Jekyll and Hyde. Pain, hunger and stress all have negative effects on our resilience. The majority of us are more resilient on a Monday at the beginning of term than a Friday near the end of term. So, when talking about resilience make sure you include support networks and recognise it is not constant.

I will use the word *resilience* in this book, as it is linked to self-esteem. But, please remember what I mean by resilience – the ability to believe in yourself and recognise your strengths and weaknesses. To have internal and external resources to support you through your difficult times. It's not just about being able to cope with failing an exam or being okay with criticism.

Factors for resilience

AKA Good self-esteem is resilience (are you picking up on this yet?)

Positive self-esteem is crucial for good mental health and well-being, and newsflash: it improves learning! When training I often ask delegates what they do on a regular basis to improve the self-esteem of their pupils – not just academically. All too often staff struggle to think what they do, particularly outside of academic and sports achievements. It's a habit we get into, but also a habit we can change (*see later chapter on positive motivation*).

Believing in yourself and your abilities is so powerful. It isn't about believing you are great, better than everyone and able to conquer everything – that comes under bad positive thinking. It's about being able to recognise your strengths and weaknesses (like a bad interview question) and being OK with that. Knowing you will persevere and be OK.

Albert Ellis, one of the daddies of cognitive behavioural therapy, talks about the "three musts". These "musts" are things we tell ourselves which we tell ourselves are absolute. They can become irrational and fixed and lead to anxiety, stress, depression, anger, etc. The three musts are:

1   I must do well and win the approval of others or I am no good.
2   People must do the right thing or be punished.
3   Life must be easy.

The first one is the one that is mostly related to our self-esteem, and especially that of pupils: the "I must do well and win the approval of others or else I am no good" or "I must be successful, or I am not worthy". We each have a specific idea of what that success is. It can be a variety of things. I must:

- be rich
- be powerful
- have more money
- be thinner
- be fatter
- be more muscular
- be sportier
- be faster
- have a better car
- drive faster
- have on-fleek eyebrows (I am so on trend)
- have a bigger backside
- have a smaller backside
- not look old
- be taller and so on

There are many versions of 'successful'. For pupils their environment is all about being successful academically, which is something we can perpetuate. They believe their value and worth is directly related to their academic success: "I must get an A* or I am not worthy of love", or "If I don't pass, my life will be over". This is why we are seeing a major increase in exam anxiety. Pupils are constantly being told that they must achieve a certain standard to be worthy. This is then passed on to parents who believe that if their child doesn't achieve a certain academic standard, they are a terrible parent (discussed again later).

Good self-esteem is about liking yourself without setting yourself irrational values you must achieve to be loved. For me: I'm not perfect but I like my quirks and characteristics. Not everyone likes me but that's OK. It's my value of success that counts, not yours.

And that's what one of the major parts of resilience is: liking yourself and helping pupils to like themselves for who they are. That's why we have to help raise self-esteem in pupils: so they can like themselves for who they are and not be hostage to irrational expectations that actually don't mean much in later life. Eyebrows are important but I've not seen one gravestone that had "She had great eyebrows" engraved on it. Yet. (I don't like my eyebrows btw.)

I regularly ask staff and pupils I am speaking to, to tell me one thing about themselves they like. The number that struggle with it is saddening. And it's not bragging because we aren't saying I am better than you at it. We are saying I like this about myself and that's good. Everyone should be able to like themselves.

The importance of friendships

AKA Support networks are a big part of resilience and self-esteem

As we mentioned earlier, resilience isn't just about what is within you, it's also about who is around you. I mentioned earlier about my fabulous support network. I have the best support network and for that I am grateful. My first husband was stupid enough to leave me (I know you're shocked how stupid he was to do that, but I am glad he did now) and that was hard. Fortunately, my support network helped me through the difficult time – emotionally, physically and financially.

My support network wasn't just about family, it was also about my friends. A big part of having a support network is our friendships. Friendships are very important to pupils and very important to resilience.

- I am lucky to have a supportive family; not everyone has that.
- We can all develop supportive friendship groups.

Van Harmelen et al.[1] found that "[f]riendship and family support were positive predictors of immediate resilient PSF [psychosocial functioning], with friendship support being the strongest predictor". As a result, they suggested that "[i]nterventions that promote the skills needed to acquire and sustain adolescent friendships may be crucial in increasing adolescent resilient PSF".

Improving resilience isn't just about boosting individual self-esteem but also about supporting friendship groups. As education professionals we have a major part to play in this. Later, I suggest ideas to promote friendships, but again, one of the key factors is what we model.

Hendrickx et al.[2] studied teacher support and conflict, and peer ecologies. They found that "the teacher functions as a model or social referent for students regarding how to interact and form relationships with others. When teachers are aware of this, they can deliberately use their everyday interactions with students as network-related teaching strategies". We can positively promote friendships and improve resilience.

This is further supported by Hughes, Cavell and Willson,[3] who found that classmates make inferences on attributes and likeability based, in part, on observations of teacher interactions. Again, this is further evidence to support modelling and emphasise our influence on mental health and well-being.

The value of friendships can also be seen in one of the common factors in mental health issues – social isolation. We all need interaction with others. As mentioned earlier, maintaining social interaction (and chocolate) is a major part of how I manage my depression. When I go out and laugh, I feel better and always end up saying "We should do that more often". So, I plan it and make sure I do it more often.

Value all success

AKA Recognise more than academic results

Everybody knows that self-confidence affects performance. It improves it. We can get too focused on resilience being about being able to deal with crap. But resilience and self-esteem are also about believing in yourself and wanting to improve. There's a whole chapter on positive reinforcement later which will go into this aspect in more detail.

Unfortunately, as we've already identified, the education system can go against improving self-belief and self-esteem. We use language such as "below expectations", we are always talking about what the next goal is, we set minimum acceptable standards regardless of the ability of the child. We label children from an early age and set them accordingly. If they do well, we put them up a set, so they go from being top ability in one set (improving confidence) to bottom of the next set (potentially damaging confidence). I'm not going to debate setting, but I just want to mention the big-fish-little-pond effect discussed by Marsh, H, Kong, C.K & Hau, K.T (2000). They found that "[i]t is better for academic self-concept to be a big fish in a little pond (gifted student in regular reference group) than to be a small fish in a big pond (gifted student in gifted reference group)". Also, the Education Endowment Foundation found that setting by ability had a negative effect on academic progress.[5]

Now, obviously not everyone can be a big fish in a little pond, and I am sure that ability 'setting' will be here for some time. However, we have to be aware of the implications of it and try to counteract these. These include implications on an individual's self-esteem and self-belief and the effect on mental health and well-being. We must talk about there being a range of skills and talents – that we are good in some areas and not so much in others and that is okay. That one talent isn't valued higher than another. Whilst the academic system is set up to measure academic ability, we must ensure that it is not the only thing we measure and reward. Success in life does not just come from achieving good exam results. There is a whole world outside exams and education – honestly!

An article from *Forbes Magazine*[6] identifies research that shows 80% of financial success is down to personality and communication skills. It further identifies a psychologist who shows that people would rather do business with someone they like, not because they got a high grade in their English GCSE. Now, I'm not saying qualifications aren't important; they are for many people and careers. But not for everybody and they are not the only measure. We have to remember this. As I write this book the UK education system currently requires pupils to have a Level 2 Maths and English qualification to undertake an apprenticeship such as plumbing or plastering. This is just crazy and elitism at work again.

I have previously mentioned self-determination theory, which is a theory of motivation and I am a big fan. It believes that there are three key elements for healthy development and functioning. Some say these are the three elements to happiness. They are relatedness, autonomy and competence. Autonomy is a whole other discussion not for this book and we have already discussed the importance of relationships for our mental well-being. The third one is competence – the need and importance of achieving and building competence in an area that is important to them. We must not assume this is academic for all pupils and we must provide opportunities for them to achieve competence in the area they choose. Howard and Johnson,[7] when talking about resilience, explain that schools should expand the range of ways that pupils can demonstrate achievement to improve resilience. We shouldn't ignore academic targets and results, as that is one of our aims. But this must not be the only area of recognition and encouragement.

Working within the constraints of the education system

AKA But Sam, that's how the system is set up

I have acknowledged several times that we are measured on exam results and they are important. But they are not the be all and end all, and we don't have to focus solely on those. Ironically, by focusing on good mental well-being (and taking all the fabulous advice in this book), you will improve results as a result of improving mental health and well-being. Dix et al.[8] showed a significant link between implementation of a quality whole-school mental health promotion and improving academic performance. When we apply for jobs, we are not appointed purely based on our exam results. We are interviewed and appointed on our qualities – yes, there is a minimum, but that is often overlooked for the 'right person'.

As education professionals ourselves we can be guilty of perpetuating the academic-focus obsession. When we have conversations with people who have children, we always ask what are they doing, where are they studying, what grades did they get, what do they want to do, etc. We judge our parenting ability on the academic success of a child; we rarely ask if they are happy. Do they laugh a lot? Do they have good friends? Are they kind? Are these not more important values?

The area in which I live still has the grammar system, and for many, the grammar school is something to work towards and achieve. It is incorrectly seen as a superior form of education (controversial there, Sam). I hate the 11+ results day each year. It becomes a toxic environment of parents and pupils comparing and rating each other to see if they 'got in'. A friend of mine was approached in Sainsbury's (other supermarkets are available) by a lady saying how sorry she was that she heard her daughter hadn't passed the 11+ and how disappointed they must have been. My friend showed great restraint by not punching her in the face, but this is how obsessional and judgemental of children we have become.

I recently had an operation and recognised one of the theatre nurses. Our children had gone to school together. We talked about what our children are doing, and she was almost apologetic that her son had completed his degree but was only working as a lifeguard at a local holiday park. Why apologise? That's great and if he's happy, good for him! He's saving lives – I value that quite highly!

We have to reinforce the message that academic results are one measure of a person but not the only measure. And the value of a pupil is not decided by the results. Ever. We value all pupils and if we want to improve mental well-being and resilience, we have to boost self-esteem of all pupils, to recognise all their qualities and talents. I don't know anyone who asks for a CV and exam certificates before deciding whether to be friends with someone. "Sorry, I'm looking for a best friend who got an A in Maths, and that just isn't you! If you retake and get a higher grade, let me know".

There may be some of you thinking; it's all a bit rubbish and we have to be critical sometimes to motivate pupils. You should check out the later chapter on positive reinforcement.

Boosting self-esteem

AKA Again, put your money where your mouth is then, Garner

We have to provide multiple opportunities for all children to thrive, demonstrate their talents and be recognised – not just in those areas that will be valued by external inspectors. We value a wide range of skills and abilities. Here are some suggestions as to the ways we can boost self-esteem, followed by some CBT activities that can be completed individually or with groups:

Have a range of clubs

Not just PE- or music-/drama-based. Think cookery, knitting, Warhammer, gaming, Film Club, Chess Club. Even a Getting Your Eyebrows Right Club (I may be obsessed with eyebrows). Older pupils or external volunteers can run the clubs. It also promotes skills and friendships.

N.B. *And please don't use these clubs as another excuse to get a qualification or certificate. I'm sure some of you thought "Oh yes, we can do that as part of the Duke of Edinburgh Award, or the Seagull Certificate of Niceness" (I made that one up by the way). But you can do things just because they're fun or good. We don't always have to achieve a qualification or certificate out of it.*

Recognise achievements outside of school

Ask parents and pupils to let you know of achievements/interests outside of school. You could have a Judo champion in your midst and not know it. A pupil who volunteers at the local animal shelter. A pupil who is really good at baking (I definitely recommend finding this one out). Acknowledge their achievements in assembly, class, etc. It doesn't always have to be a certificate, just a 'shout-out'.

Tea and Cakes or Hot Chocolate Friday

I used to invite pupils to have tea and cake with me once a week and talk about them, get to know them. Many schools have embraced Hot Chocolate Friday where pupils are nominated to have hot chocolate on Friday with the head teacher for differing positive reasons. (Side note: Perhaps we could do this with staff but call it Vodka Friday Evening?)

Remember small details

I am always flattered when people remember my name (especially my husband). It means a lot to me, genuinely. Children are the same. Remember little details and ask them about it. Take time to ask about events and follow up. I suggest later using form/tutor time for activities like this.

Acknowledge every pupil

A wise and fabulous woman once told me to always acknowledge pupils and I have carried this with me since, and do the same with adults. It works. You don't have to say hello to every pupil, but those you know let them know you see them, and that they exist. A nod of the head or hello, a smile – these go a long way to letting a pupil know they matter, and that is good for self-esteem.

Don't use pupil events to 'inspire achievement'

Events should be open to all regardless, not just for those who achieve a certain attendance or academic level. I'm not a fan of attendance certificates – it's actually a fluke most of the time that they didn't get ill that year and isn't something other children can work towards. Alternatively, they may have had a nurse for a mother (like my fabulous sister) who doesn't believe anyone is ill unless their leg is hanging off, and then they just need a plaster! So often staff would complain 'naughty' pupils were being rewarded by attending an activity. Activities are important for all pupils. Also, as we will see in the positive motivation chapter, they improve motivation and positive relationships. Many of these pupils have had poor life experiences, so don't begrudge them a positive one.

Look at your school reporting system

What is it based on? What language do you use? Is it deficit-based using negative language? Do you report on strengths? How can this be improved to boost self-esteem? Does a mark for effort really boost self-esteem? Grade A for effort and Grade F for achievement doesn't make me feel better about myself. Again, this is covered further in the positive reinforcement chapter.

Start every day/each lesson with a compliment

At the start of all my training/presenting, I always ask delegates to pay each other a compliment and respond "Thank you, you're right". It feels unnatural at first but always boosts self-esteem and makes people smile. Try it. There are lots of videos on YouTube where teachers welcome pupils with a handshake into the classroom. It makes a difference.

Self-esteem pupil focus by staff

If a pupil is particularly struggling with self-esteem, ask all staff to take opportunities to boost their self-esteem wherever possible over the next few weeks. How they feel about themselves, and how others see them will improve. I've seen it done; it's amazing and so simple. It would also help to improve their social standing.

Have personal accountability

Ask yourself daily or weekly, what did I do to boost the self-esteem of all my pupils this week? What can I do next week? It all builds positive relationships which improve learning.

Chapter summary

- Low self-esteem is the most common factor in mental health issues.
- Self-esteem affects resilience.
- Resilience isn't just about internal factors and is fluid.
- Support networks are crucial for resilience.
- Friendship groups are important to pupils.
- Provide a range of opportunities to achieve and excel.
- Value all success, not just academic.
- Value all children.

Supporting tools and activities

PROMOTING FRIENDSHIPS

As well as modelling positive social interaction, there are specific activities that can be undertaken to help pupils develop friendship skills.

Whole-class activities

Have discussions about:

- what makes a good friend
- how people make friends

- how to resolve arguments between friends
- trying to look at the other person's point of view

Small-group activities

For pupils who may be socially isolated or struggle with making friends you could run regular small groups. Think of a positive name for the group: not the "Billy No Mates Group", but something like "Friends Group". Activities should be discussion-led and cover areas such as:

- how to make friends
- what makes you a good friend
- what to say when someone says something you don't like
- how to be considerate of other people's feelings
- improving social skills – role play and modelling
- what clubs and activities they could join in your setting
- activities to improve self-esteem which will boost friendship skills

You may wish to use social stories or set up role-play situations such as going shopping or meeting new people.

Learning to resolve friendship disagreements

What happened?	What is my point of view?	What is their point of view?	Is it worth losing a friendship over?	What can I do to resolve/fix this?	What am I going to do next?	What have I learned from this?

Learning to resolve friendship disagreements – Example worksheet

Question	Response
What happened?	Claire and I had an argument about her always talking about herself
What is my point of view?	That she is never interested in me. It's a one-way friendship
What is their point of view?	That I'm being unfair and she is a good friend and she does talk about me as well
Is it worth losing a friendship over?	No.
What can I do to resolve/fix this?	Compromise? Accept I'm feeling low.
What am I going to do next?	Speak to Claire. Apologise for my part and tell her I need some support at the moment
What have I learned from this?	That when I am down maybe I see things more negatively.

Boosting self-esteem CBT activity

Things I am good at	
What I like about myself	
Nice things other people say about me	
People in my life I am grateful for	
What makes me laugh	

Boosting self-esteem CBT activity – Example worksheet

Things I am good at	Singing Laughing Talking to people
What I like about myself	I am approachable I don't judge I am optimistic
Nice things other people say about me	That I am funny I have a nice smile I am easy to talk to I am a good singer
People in my life I am grateful for	Family Husband Friends
What makes me laugh	Cat videos People falling over French and Saunders

References

1   Van Harmelen, A.L et al (2017). *Adolescent Friendships Predict Later Resilient Functioning Across Psychosocial Domains in a Healthy Community Cohort.* Cambridge: Wellcome Trust.

2   Hendrickx, M, Mainhard, T, Boor-Klip, H.J, Cillessen, A & Brekelmans, M (2016). Social Dynamics in the Classroom: Teacher Support and Conflict and the Peer Ecology. *Teaching and Teacher Education.* 53: 30–40. doi: 10.1016/j.tate.2015.10.004

3   Hughes, J.N, Cavell, T.A & Willson, V (2001). Further Support for the Developmental Significance of the Quality of the Teacher – Student Relationship. *Texas A&M University: Journal of School Psychology.*39, 4 ed.

4   Marsh, H, Kong, C.K & Hau, K.T (2000). Longitudinal Multilevel Models of the Big-Fish-Little-Pond Effect on Academic Self-Concept: Counterbalancing Contrast and Reflected-Glory Effects in Hong Kong Schools. *Journal of Personality and Social Psychology.* 78: 337–49. doi: 10.1037/0022-3514.78.2.337

5   Education Endowment Foundation (2018). *Setting or Streaming.* [Online]. England: Education Endowment Foundation. [26 April 2019]. Available from: https://edu cationendowmentfoundation.org.uk/evidence-summaries/teaching-learning-toolkit/setting-or-streaming/#closeSignup

6   Jensen, K (2012). *Intelligence Is Overrated: What You Really Need To Succeed.* [Online]. USA: Forbes. [26 April 2019]. Available from: www.forbes.com/sites/keldjensen/2012/04/12/intelligence-is-overrated-what-you-really-need-to-succeed/#15672c1ab6d2

7   Howard, S & Johnson, B (2000). *Resilient and Non-Resilient Behaviour in Adolescents.* Trends & Issues in Crime and Criminal Justice No. 183. Canberra: Australian Institute of Criminology. Available from: https://aic.gov.au/publications/tandi/tandi183

8   Dix, K.L, Slee, P.T, Lawson, M.J & Keeves, J.P (2012), Implementation Quality of Whole-School Mental Health Promotion and Students' Academic Performance. *Child and Adolescent Mental Health.* 17: 45–51. doi: 10.1111/j.1475-3588.2011.00608.x

Chapter 3

Bullying

Address bullying

AKA Don't pretend it doesn't happen in your setting

Bullying has serious consequences on the mental health of young people, and these are often long-term. Almost every educational setting will have bullying. Any setting that denies this is just not aware of it. The key is how the setting manages bullying.

There are plenty of statistics available regarding the amount of bullying that takes place – it's too high. The Department for Education research[1] showed 40% of children had been bullied in the last twelve months. 21% daily. And this leads to absence, exclusions and truancy amongst other things. Actual violence was more likely to take place in school.

The National Child Development Study looked at the lives of a group of people who were born in England, Scotland and Wales in 1958. They found 28% had been bullied and 15% bullied frequently. So, we don't seem to have got any better at reducing bullying. We're maybe better at talking about it.

The key issue is the impact of bullying on mental health. The said National Child Development Study[2] found that "[i]ndividuals who were bullied in childhood were more likely to have poorer physical and psychological health and cognitive functioning at age 50. Individuals who were frequently bullied in childhood were at an increased risk of depression, anxiety disorders, and suicidal thoughts".

Bullying has a big impact on mental health. I have already mentioned how low self-esteem and social isolation are common factors in many mental health issues. There's also a third – ruminative negative thinking. Bullying has an impact on all three. It affects relationships and self-confidence. If we feel powerless to stop it and believe the bullies, we develop ruminative negative thinking. These are direct impacts on mental well-being. And it happens across all demographics and all settings. This chapter isn't in-depth about preventing bullying; that's a whole book and there are lots of great organisations who provide advice about preventing bullying. This chapter is about understanding the impacts of bullying and asking you to look at how to deal with it in your setting.

What is bullying?

AKA But Sam, the term *bully* is bandied around too much

Whenever I talk about bullying and the impacts of it on mental health, I often get comments saying "Well, it's not really bullying most of the time" and "They do bandy that word about so easily now". There must be a strong definition of bullying recognised by all staff, parents and pupils and settings should work with pupils to decide on their definition of bullying. In my opinion (any many others), it is repetitive harmful behaviour where there is an imbalance of power, physical or otherwise, and perceived or real. There may not be an obvious imbalance, but it could be there, and careful exploration is needed. Bullying can be physical, verbal, cyberbullying or relational. Relational bullying is the act of spreading rumours or specifically excluding a pupil from events/social groups etc.

This doesn't mean that when we feel bullying isn't taking place, as claimed by the pupil/parents, we shouldn't still provide support. The pupil is still in distress and will need support to resolve friendship issues – remember how important friendships are to resilience. (Don't forget the CBT activity to help resolve friendship arguments in the previous chapter.)

When we talk about bullying, we often talk about the bully and the victim. Luke Roberts, a fabulous expert in conflict resolution, says this language isn't helpful as it can perpetuate the bullying and label 'victims' (I will discuss labelling later). We should use the terms *perpetrator* and *target*, so that is the language I now use.

Recognising the impact

AKA It's not part of growing up

There was a TV programme on a while ago where school perpetrators of bullying faced their target to apologise 30–40 years later. I can't find it now or remember the title, but it stuck with me as a very powerful programme. The targets still remembered the trauma and it had affected them throughout their life. Receiving an apology and being told, by the perpetrator, that it wasn't their fault, had a major emotional impact. It was also cathartic for the perpetrator who had felt guilty for all that time for being the perpetrator. All those years later it was still affecting both parties. Many of you will remember an incident where you were bullied at school and the impact it had, and still may have.

The Lancet published a study claiming that, for children, bullying has a more detrimental long-term effect on mental health than being neglected.[3] This study has received criticism, but there is no doubt being the victim of bullying is majorly damaging to the mental health and well-being of pupils and adults. Many studies are using neuroimaging to show that emotional pain has a similar effect on the brain as physical pain.[4]

It is not part of growing up and as educators we have the responsibility to ensure we reduce bullying and limit its effects on the mental health and well-being of pupils as much as possible.

Review your bullying policy regularly

AKA Know for sure if it's working and it's not just a tick-box exercise

The vast majority of schools now have a bullying policy and like all policies, it should be reviewed regularly to ensure it is working. Often, when I ask a setting if the policy is working, I am told that reports of bullying have reduced or something similar. But not all bullying is reported, and the less effective you are at dealing with bullying the less likely it is to be reported. Unless you conduct a regular anonymous survey asking pupils about bullying, you will not know how much is taking place. Even anonymously we may not know the true data, but it will be as close as we can get. As a parent I might think that my star chart for my daughter to tidy her bedroom is working. However, in reality she is shoving all the mess under her bed, so it's not really working, just putting it out of sight. Unless you have a system where pupils can honestly give feedback about bullying, anonymously, you don't know the extent of bullying in your setting.

Often pupils won't report bullying as they worry it will become a big issue that will have to be sorted but won't really be sorted. So, they keep quiet about it. They should have the opportunity to give feedback about it and be asked if they would like help with the situation. Anonymous surveys and reporting allow this to take place. It may mean you cannot analyse each situation, and some may not be 'bullying' by the definition. But what's important is knowing whether you are effectively managing bullying in your centre, whether your policy is working. We also need to consider how we are managing the impact of bullying on targets. Are we effectively supporting them? Bullying policies shouldn't only be about the amount of bullying and how it is punished. It should also detail the follow-up and support provided.

Data from a survey has to be used when reviewing your bullying policy. All too often policies are reviewed by SLT without any consultation of any other stakeholders. I know of no other industry that doesn't consult with stakeholders (a business-speak word for customers/clients) when looking to improve their practice. Tesco wouldn't sit in the boardroom deciding customer service policy without the data from customer service feedback. Yet too often I hear of SLT reviewing the bullying policy without consultation from anyone else. Okay, so pupils aren't our clients or customers like Tesco. However, they are the main stakeholders and should be consulted. Remember, autonomy is a key element of happiness, and can affect mental health and well-being. Consultation improves the feeling of autonomy and belonging.

Being preventative

AKA Building relationships with vulnerable children in advance

Most education staff I speak to can pretty much identify pupils who will be bullying targets when they join school. It's not a nice thing to say, but it is true. Some have a 'look', some are vulnerable pupils such as SEN, some have poor social skills or are statistically more likely to be bullied, such as LGBT pupils and so on. They may have low self-esteem and high anxiety. If you can identify it, so can the perpetrator. We need to identify and work with vulnerable pupils as a preventative measure. Build positive relationships with them and help them build positive relationships with each other and make good friendship groups. Help them know how to report bullying and where to go for support.

I haven't mentioned resilience here. Resilience doesn't help with bullying. A more resilient pupil is likely to suffer bullying longer before they report it. It should be reported and dealt with immediately.

I hope that suggesting we identify and work with vulnerable pupils doesn't sound like victim blaming – that isn't my intention and we will discuss perpetrators later. It's acknowledging that some pupils are more likely to be bullying targets. Identifying those pupils and supporting them from the beginning will help their mental health and well-being, and reduce the risks of being a bullying target.

Again, we need to talk about modelling with regard to bullying. What sort of environment is your setting – is it respectful? Do you promote acceptance and understanding for everyone? Do you model this in how support staff are treated and valued or is there a strict hierarchical system? Is there a key member of staff who always deals with staff and pupil discipline? Is your setting a hierarchical system based on academic achievements? Hierarchical systems are more likely to have bullying taking place,[5] for staff and pupils. We have to model and have a system that accepts everyone for who they are – a theme that echoes previous chapters and what's to come in future chapters. Is your setting a nice place to be for everyone, or just those who fit the mould?

Acknowledge all types of bullying

AKA Teachers can be bullies too

There can also be teacher bullying. If we define bullying as repetitive harmful behaviour where there is an imbalance of power, then we have to acknowledge there is an imbalance of power between teacher and pupil that can be incorrectly used. A teacher constantly victimising a pupil who they don't like should be considered bullying. We have to acknowledge it to address it. Teachers who constantly shout or use physical intimidation (via body language or otherwise) are effectively bullying. Using threatening techniques to obtain compliance or humiliation is bullying. Again, potentially another controversial statement but, is it really? Teachers who use bullying as a tactic are normalising bullying behaviour. If you have a teacher who you can regularly hear shouting at pupils across the school, that's bullying behaviour. It certainly isn't modelling self-regulated, controlled behaviour.

Shouting at vulnerable pupils who have experienced trauma such as domestic violence, community violence, etc. is retraumatising them. It is hugely detrimental to their mental well-being. They will remain in a state of hypervigilance and no learning will take place. It's about treating children as human beings. I am using strong language here because I do feel strongly about this and there are many who disagree, possibly as that means accepting that they may have been mentally harmed pupils themselves. Yes, I have shouted at pupils in the past, but it was mostly when I was stressed, and I often apologised after. Apologising, by the way, is modelling positive behaviour – acknowledging I made a mistake, that I was stressed, and it was about me not them. I also wasn't aware of how I was retraumatising already traumatised pupils. I do now. It may be where language is important. If we replace "pupil" with "child", does that make you feel differently? Pupils are children, after all.

How do you deal with bullying?

AKA Do you just bollock the perpetrator then move on?

We often dismiss bullying as we don't know how to deal with it or are unable to stop it. We suggest things like staying away from them or blocking them on social media – but this isn't effective or helpful. As part of your bullying policy have a flexible procedure for dealing with bullying to accommodate all types of scenarios – online, face to face, scenarios where the pupil does want action taken, etc. Also, ensure that the way you deal with bullying doesn't make the target feel more of a victim and less empowered.

Some settings use restorative justice for bullying. Evidence has shown that restorative justice can have a very positive impact on behaviour, attendance, etc., when used correctly. However, many settings aren't using restorative justice correctly and are cherry-picking bits to suit. Restorative justice is a process and a whole-school process. It's not just about having quick conversations and that's it. Make sure it is the appropriate approach and then used correctly. Where there is a large imbalance of power, or the target has very low self-esteem, there is a possibility the restorative justice approach could be more damaging than helpful. Always ask the target's permission first and explain what will happen in advance.

Shouting at perpetrators as a punishment is not effective. It normalises bullying – see the teacher bullying above. The perpetrator is likely bullying for a reason – often linked to self-esteem and mental well-being. In order to make effective change we need to address these issues, so a combination of consequence and support to change future behaviour should be used. There are CBT activities at the end of this chapter that can be used with the perpetrator to help change bullying behaviour.

Support the target after bullying

AKA It's not just about stopping it

As previously mentioned, it's important that we support targets to reduce the impacts on their mental health in the short and long term. It should go without saying that we never ignore bullying and should always deal with it. One of the long-term effects of bullying is lack of trust in people. By ignoring bullying as educators, we are also sending a message to pupils that people in authority cannot be trusted. This could affect them in the future when dealing with police, medical staff, etc.[6]

To support the target after bullying, we have to look at the main areas of mental well-being that are affected. These are self-esteem, negative thinking, self-blame, and feeling socially isolated – all the common factors in mental health issues. Pupils are likely to believe they are worthless, that their future is hopeless, no one likes them. They may also have frustration at not being able to express their anger. Repressed anger is dangerous for our mental and physical health.[7]

There are CBT activities at the end of this chapter that address these areas to help reduce the long-term impact of being bullied. As with all CBT, it needs to be practised to become habit.

We also need to help targets have a 'plan' of what to do if they are bullied again – remember much anxiety is based on fear of the unknown, helping pupils have a plan of what to do in a situation will reduce anxiety and support feelings of control. Remember, autonomy is one of the elements of happiness. It all links up!

So, what should we do?

AKA Usual money-where-mouth-is stuff, Garner

Regularly survey pupils

Suggested questions are in the supporting tools and activities at the end of the chapter.

Think about unstructured times

A lot of bullying takes place during unstructured times such as break time. Provide a safe place for pupils to go during these times – a supervised classroom or lunch club. This should be a basic in all schools for all vulnerable pupils.

Support social skills

Very many pupils struggle with social skills (not just PE teachers). We should provide a social skills group to help pupils learn the etiquette of social interaction and basically, how to make friends. It doesn't come naturally to everyone. There were activities for this in the previous chapter.

Have a wide range of clubs and groups

I mentioned this during self-esteem, and it is important here. Providing social support networks and a sense of identity will help targets lessen their vulnerability.

Chapter summary

- Acknowledge bullying in your setting.
- Bullying has a major long-term impact on mental health of pupils.
- How you manage and follow up bullying is the important factor.
- Have a strong definition of bullying.
- Pupils must be consulted in regular bullying-policy reviews.
- Vulnerable pupils should be supported proactively.
- Bullying behaviour must not be normalised by staff.
- Therapeutic work must be undertaken with the target to reduce the effect of bullying on mental health.
- Therapeutic measures should be used with the perpetrator to effectively change behaviour.
- A safe place should be provided during unstructured times for vulnerable pupils.

Supporting tools and activities

BULLYING QUESTIONNAIRE

- What is bullying?
- Have you ever been bullied?
- Have you been bullied in this school/setting?
- When was the last time you were bullied?

- Was the bully/perpetrator older than you?
- Did other people see the bullying?
- Where did it happen?
- What did the bully do?
- How did it make you feel?
- Did you report the bullying, and if so, who to?
- If not, why not?
- If yes, what did that person do?
- Do you think this will stop the bullying?
- Is there anything else we could have done?
- Are there any school/setting activities you don't do because you are worried about being bullied?
- Have you ever bullied someone?
- What did you do?
- Why did you do it?
- How did you feel afterwards?
- Do you know someone who is being bullied but who isn't reporting it?
- Do you know why they won't report it?
- Do we do enough to stop bullying in the school/setting?
- What more could we do about bullying?
- Are you bullied anywhere else outside school/setting?
- Is there anything you would like to say about bullying?

Target support activity

Being a target is distressing. We must acknowledge and discuss these emotions. These are conversation starters to use with targets following an 'incident'. Remember to listen and acknowledge before exploring more positive thoughts. You may also like use these with small groups of 'targets' who are able to support each other and realise they are not alone.

What did the other pupil say/do?

How did this make you feel?

Why do you think they picked on you?

Often, pupils pick on other pupils because they are feeling bad. Do you think this could be the case with the pupil who picked on you? What could they be feeling?

Tell me about your friends in and out of school.

What do they like about you?

Would you like more friends? If so, how do you think you can do this?

What can I do to help? Are there any activities/clubs you would like to do/join?

What do you like about you?

Sometimes we start to believe the nasty things that other pupils say, even though it's not true. What could you tell yourself next time you start to have negative thoughts about yourself?

N.B. Remember we discussed asking teachers to 'big up' pupils with low self-esteem and how it can make a difference. This is also useful to do with pupils who are being bullied

Target support activity – Example answers

Being a target is distressing. We must acknowledge and discuss these emotions. These are conversation starters to use with targets following an 'incident'. Remember to listen and acknowledge before exploring more positive thoughts. You may also like use these with small groups of 'targets' who are able to support each other and realise they are not alone.

What did the other pupil say/do?

Called me stupid/ugly

How did this make you feel?

Sad, embarrassed. Ugly and stupid.

Why do you think they picked on you?

Because I am ugly/stupid. Because I am weak

Often, pupils pick on other pupils because they are feeling bad. Do you think this could be the case with the pupil who picked on you? What could they be feeling?

They could be feeling sad or angry.

Tell me about your friends in and out of school.

John plays xBox with me. Michael lives in my road. We play football. That's it really

What do they like about you?

I am nice. I am good at football and gaming

Would you like more friends? If so, how do you think you can do this?

Yes. Maybe I could join a club?

What can I do to help? Are there any activities/clubs you would like to do/join?

Yes. Help me join a club and know what to do please

What do you like about you?

I am nice. I am good at gaming.

Sometimes we start to believe the nasty things that other pupils say, even though it's not true. What could you tell yourself next time you start to have negative thoughts about yourself?

That it isn't true. That they are saying things because they feel bad. That I am a nice person, not ugly or stupid

N.B. Remember we discussed asking teachers to 'big up' pupils with low self-esteem and how it can make a difference. This is also useful to do with pupils who are being bullied

Target support plan

Let's come up with a plan of what you will do in the future if you are picked on by another pupil. You will need to practise this in your head to help you feel more prepared.

Where and when is it most likely to happen?

Why do you think it is more likely to happen there and then?

Is there anything you could do in advance to make it less likely to happen?

Thinking about how pupils are less likely to pick on other pupils if they don't react, how will you act and what will you say to the pupil if it happens again?

Could you pretend you didn't hear or see them?

What will you tell yourself afterwards?

Who will you speak to afterwards, if it happens again?

Target support plan – Example answers

Let's come up with a plan of what you will do in the future if you are picked on by another pupil. You will need to practise this in your head to help you feel more prepared.

Where and when is it most likely to happen?

During lunch and break times

Why do you think it is more likely to happen there and then?

Cos no teachers watching

Is there anything you could do in advance to make it less likely to happen?

I don't know. Maybe ask him on his own not to do it

Thinking about how pupils are less likely to pick on other pupils if they don't react, how will you act and what will you say to the pupil if it happens again?

I will ignore him and walk away

Could you pretend you didn't hear or see them?

I will try

What will you tell yourself afterwards?

That I am a nice person and people like me. That it is about him not me

Who will you speak to afterwards, if it happens again?

You Miss

Supporting positive behaviour change for the perpetrator

Adult led conversation:

What happened recently with …?

Why do you think you said or did that?

Were there other people watching?

How did it make you feel?

How do you think it made the other pupil feel?

How would you feel if somebody did that to one of your friends or relatives?

Tell me some things that you like about yourself…

What makes you feel happy?

What makes you feel angry and/or sad?

Is this when you feel like picking on other pupils?

Do you think that's a good way of dealing with feeling sad and/or angry?

Supporting positive behaviour change for the perpetrator – Example answers

Adult led conversation:

What happened recently with …?

I called him ugly and stupid

Why do you think you said or did that?

Because I don't like him.

Were there other people watching?

Yes

How did it make you feel?

People laughed so I felt good

How do you think it made the other pupil feel?

Sad maybe

How would you feel if somebody did that to one of your friends or relatives?

I would be really angry

Tell me some things that you like about yourself…

I am good at sport

What makes you feel happy?

Laughing with my mates

What makes you feel angry and/or sad?

When people think I am stupid

Is this when you feel like picking on other pupils?

Maybe. I think people expect it from me

Do you think that's a good way of dealing with feeling sad and/or angry?

Not really

What could you do to make yourself feel better when you feel angry or sad?

Go and talk to someone about it or go and write/draw

What do you think will be the consequences if you keep picking on the other pupil?

I'll keep getting into trouble and have to leave school

Is that what you would like to happen?

Possibly but probably not. I'd miss my friends, but it would nebe nice to not to come to school

Could you tell me some good things about the other pupil?

They're quite funny

What will you do next time you see the other pupil?

Ignore them

What could you do to make yourself feel better when you feel angry or sad?

Go and play with mates

What do you think will be the consequences if you keep picking on the other pupil?

I will get in to trouble

Is that what you would like to happen?

Don't care. Not really

Could you tell me some good things about the other pupil?

He's good at football

What will you do next time you see the other pupil?

I will ignore him or say hello

References

1   Lessof, C et al (2016). *Longitudinal Study of Young People in England Cohort 2: Health and Wellbeing at Wave 2.* [Online]. England: DFE. [1 May 2019]. Available from: https://assets.publishing.service.gov.uk/government/uploads/system/uploads/attachment_data/file/599871/LSYPE2_w2-research_report.pdf

2   Takizawa, R, Maughan, B & Arseneault, L (2014). *Adult Health Outcomes of Childhood Bullying Victimization: Evidence from a 5-Decade Longitudinal British Birth Cohort.* [Online]. USA: American Journal of Psychiatry. [1 May 2019]. Available from: www.kcl.ac.uk/ioppn/news/records/2014/April/Impact-of-childhood-bullying-still-evident-after-40-years

3   Lereya, S.T et al (2015). *Adult Mental Health Consequences of Peer Bullying and Maltreatment in Childhood: Two Cohorts in Two Countries.* [Online]. England: The Lancet. [1 May 2019]. Available from: www.thelancet.com/journals/lanpsy/article/PIIS2215-0366(15)00165-0/fulltext

4   Eisenberger, N.I, Lieberman, M & Williams, K.D (2003). Does Rejection Hurt? An fMRI Study of Social Exclusion. *Science* (New York, NY). 302: 290–2. doi: 10.1126/science.1089134

5   Garandeau, C.F, Lee, I.A & Salmivalli, C (2014). Inequality Matters: Classroom Status Hierarchy and Adolescents' Bullying. USA: Springer US. *Journal of Youth Adolescence.* 43: 1123. [1 May 2019]. https://doi.org/10.1007/s10964-013-0040-4

6   Wolke, D et al (2013). *Impact of Bullying in Childhood on Adult Health, Wealth, Crime, and Social Outcomes.* [Online]. USA: Psychological Science. [1 May 2019]. Available from: www.ncbi.nlm.nih.gov/pubmed/23959952

7   Bergland, C (2013). *Cortisol: Why the "Stress Hormone" Is Public Enemy No 1.* [Online]. (Psychology Today ed.). USA. [1 May 2019]. Available from: www.psychologytoday.com/us/blog/the-athletes-way/201301/cortisol-why-the-stress-hormone-is-public-enemy-no-1

Chapter 4

Pupil experience

Research shows that belonging is important to mental health

AKA We all need to feel that we belong to a 'tribe'

We all need to belong in our life. We want to belong at work, to family, to a friendship group, to a club, etc. I feel I belong in my family, with my friends, with fellow supporters at Gloucester Rugby Club (who are the best fans in the world obviously). We don't all have family we can belong to, but that can be substituted with 'non-blood' family. The key is belonging to something and someone. People are happier when they feel they belong. It's no different at school – for staff and pupils. We have already talked about belonging being one of the three elements of happiness from self-determination theory. Research shows that the more pupils feel they belong to a school, the better they do academically and socially.[1]

In order for pupils to belong in the school setting, we have to look at their experience in our settings. The experience of the pupil in your school will affect their sense of belonging, which is why I've called this chapter "Pupil experience", not "Pupil belonging". It's a collection of little things to think about that affect the feeling of belonging and therefore our mental health and well-being, but aren't enough to have a chapter all to themselves. They would be chapters like many of my uni assignments – padded out with crap just to hit the word count.

First impressions count

AKA Get it right from the start

I have a friend who is classed as an Old Aged Pensioner (so basically, he is old). On his first day of term he was shouted at in the playground for not wearing a blazer – humiliated and singled out on his first day. He was 11 years old; a child. This memory is still with him now and it is not a good memory. Suffice to say he hated that teacher and school for the rest of his days. He left at 16 with no qualifications. That first day set the scene for the rest of his time at school.

How you treat pupils on their first visits to school will set the tone for the rest of their experience. There is lots of research on how fast we make judgements on other people ranging from 1/10th of a second to 60 seconds. It isn't long. It's the same for pupils first experience of your setting. Think of how nervous they will be, how scary it all is moving to the next chapter of their life. We need to be understanding, nurturing, welcoming, to create a positive first impression. Unfortunately, this isn't the case in many settings. Every September I read of some head teacher who has decided to set the 'tone of respect' on the first day and send all pupils home, or isolate them, if there is a slight infringement on the uniform regulations. The very first day. The belief that this sets the tone for the rest of the school time is right – but it's not a good tone. Shouting at, humiliating and isolating a pupil when they are vulnerable and anxious is not good for mental health and well-being. It's not good for fostering achievement or creating a positive sense of belonging to the school.

Sometimes this happens before the first day of term. It can happen on transition days. I have experienced the 'inclusion' lead in the school deciding that all pupils who were attending transition day, with a reputation for being 'challenging', would be managed by him. His confrontational style meant that some had already been excluded by lunchtime. I believe this was the goal, as "We don't want children like that!"

If you want to build positive relationships and a sense of belonging that will positively impact mental well-being and results, look at how you welcome new pupils. Imagine your first day on a job where you were humiliated and reprimanded. I wouldn't be staying. In fact, I did leave a job in the first week once because I was told I "shouldn't be friendly with the software designers because they have to concentrate on their work", after I had said "Hello" and asked their names. This was a not a working environment I wanted to be in.

Transition is important

AKA It's a complicated process that needs careful management

Making good first impressions means that your transition process has to be a positive experience. Transition is a huge time of uncertainty and anxiety for many pupils which impact their mental health and well-being. Research shows that transition into a new school is important for mental health. At age 15, pupils who had a poorer transition showed higher levels of depression and lower attainment. It also shows that vulnerable pupils experienced poorer transitions.[2]

Transition between key stages has to be managed carefully. It affects first impressions but also friendships. We can be fairly cavalier about friendships believing that "They'll make new friends". This isn't always the case. The School Transition and Adjustment Research Study (STARS) showed that[3]:

- 38% of pupils kept the same very best friend through transition
- 72% of pupils kept at least one of their three best friends
- pupils who kept the same group of friends through transition showed slightly better academic progress than those who made new friends

In acknowledgement of this there are some suggestions at the end of this chapter on how to effectively manage a successful transition and support positive mental well-being (and achievement).

Pupil voice

AKA Be interested in the opinion of all pupils

I previously mentioned the importance of listening to pupils – listening and hearing what they are saying. Pupils are our clients (yes, I know you may not agree – semantics) and we have to give them the skills to develop into successful adults. However, we don't often ask for their opinion, and we should. Being heard is important to our mental health and well-being. Pupils should be asked about policies and procedures. They should be regularly surveyed on their well-being and happiness. We have tables for achievements but never tables about well-being or pupil satisfaction. By the way, I'm not a fan of 'datacising' mental well-being, where we become obsessional about measuring it but not doing anything else. Data has its place but is not a standalone thing for managing mental health and well-being. I tried to think of an intelligent word there but failed – suggestions on a postcard please.

Think about how you are managed – and remember most people leave jobs because of bad managers.[4] As employees, we are happier if we are consulted and listened to, and it's good for our well-being. Receiving edicts from above on matters that directly affect us, without any consultation, contribute to increased stress; autonomy is important. It's the same for pupils. Mental health basics are the same for everybody. Just because they are children doesn't mean it's any different than it is for us. We want to be heard and have our viewpoint considered.

When I ask schools about pupil voice, very often I am told "Oh, we have a school council". Fab. Except often it's not. School councils very often are elected or chosen by staff. The pupils who are chosen are the most popular, the best speakers or the academic achievers (there are probably some PE types in there as well). They do not reflect the experience of all pupils, particularly the most statistically vulnerable. The pupil council demographics should represent the demographics of the school – including SEN, English as an Additional Language (EAL), Looked After Children (LAC), ethnic minorities, LGBT pupils, different sexes, religions, etc. School councils should be representative of all pupils. It's like having an all-male panel who discuss and make decisions on women's health (real-life example that annoys me immensely).

The pupil council or group should also be consulted on a wide range of issues, not just "what meals would you like to see in the canteen". This is not true consultation, it's lip service. If you want to support pupil mental well-being, give them an option to be heard, and fairly represented.

Physical activity is important to mental health

AKA Why do so many pupils dislike PE?

Exercise/physical activity is good for our mental well-being. Great. Lots of evidence. So Sam, I am then asked, why isn't PE a good experience for so many pupils in school? My blunt answer is because of how we run it (and PE teachers are in charge of it). PE teachers are great, and I have worked with some fabulous ones, some of my closest friends are PE teachers, blah, blah. But in my experience, they can have a mentality of "Sport is good for everyone, we all love sport, every sport, it's great, sweating is great", etc. and that everyone should just get on with it. The way PE is run hasn't moved on much since I did PE in school over 10 years ago (OK, closer to 40 years ago.) The only thing that seems to have changed is that pupils don't have to have the two-second shower at the end of each session.

Side note – I am not a sports person. I am a creative musical person who doesn't like sweating, nor do they make a strong enough bra for me to exercise. So, I acknowledge I do have some cognitive bias in this part. Just a little.

For many adults and pupils PE was, and is, a time of humiliation and embarrassment that is detrimental to mental health and well-being rather than having the positive effect it should have. We need to look at how we 'run' PE lessons, and I make some suggestions at the end of this chapter on how to improve the PE experience for those pupils who struggle: reduce the humiliation and damage to self-esteem and increase the enjoyment factor. Key elements are staff emotional literacy and choice, and an understanding of how we can make the PE experience better for vulnerable and SEN pupils. That is, shouting at the Autistic Spectrum Disorder (ASD) pupil that he is letting his teammates down isn't appropriate (yes, that really happened).

Reward systems

AKA How effective are they?

There are many pitfalls to reward systems and I've seen limited evidence to their success. I've seen more evidence that they don't work, they demotivate pupils and they have negative consequences.[5] Reward systems can dramatically affect self-esteem in a negative way. They can also affect pupil perceptions of other pupils and therefore friendship groups. They are difficult to implement consistently across the school and day-to-day by the same member of staff. Our own mental health and well-being also has an impact. I would probably give out loads of rewards on a Monday morning when I loved everyone. Then by end of Friday I would have taken them all back! Also, as someone who likes pupils, I would probably give out more than someone who isn't so keen on them (ooh, another controversial statement).

Ask for pupil input into your reward system. Keep data on them to ensure that the distribution of rewards in your setting isn't subconsciously discriminating against a vulnerable group of pupils such as SEN or EAL. We've already discussed the importance of not just recognising academic achievements – this is just as true for reward systems. I'm not saying we should give rewards to pupils for anything: "Well done for keeping your eyes open in the lesson", or for doing something they should have: "Oh, thanks so much for helping *clear up the mess you made*". We must ensure it's not just academic motivation; that *all* pupils can earn rewards.

Personally, I wouldn't have a reward system. We need to motivate pupils to learn for intrinsic reasons (good old self-determination theory again). If you're going to have a reward system, ensure that you take account of the effect on pupil self-esteem and mental well-being and consider how you are going to counteract this.

Feeling safe is important to belonging

AKA Pupils must always feel safe – physically and psychologically

Do pupils feel safe in your setting? Particularly during unstructured times? Is there a supervised room available for pupils during break times? This is really important. Some

SEN pupils really struggle during unstructured times and will need a safe haven away from noise and chaos that can lead to sensory overload. Also, other vulnerable pupils will need a safe place where they can avoid bullies or very uncomfortable *Lord of the Flies*-type situations.

Pupils should also be provided with a room/area that is a safe haven when they are distressed. If you have pupils who become overwhelmed and 'run', provide a safe place for them to run to, as this is much safer. They must be allowed to stay there until they are feeling more 'grounded' and calmer. They must never be reprimanded in this area nor should it be a punishment. It's better they are somewhere we know and safe on the premises rather than in danger outside of school. Again, this is where staff emotional literacy and understanding is important: understanding why pupils become overwhelmed and how to help them calm and regulate their emotions.

Allow some time for relationships to build

AKA Form time doesn't have to be used for a formal 'thing'

Form time (or tutor time) used to be great. Catch up on the news first thing in the morning, have a moan about the school bus being late. Calm down after lunch time and discuss who said what and how bad/great lunch was. Had a laugh and bonded with your form tutor, etc. Unfortunately, form time, in many schools, now has to be 'productive'. It is now filled with a programme or lesson-type thing, or silent reading (see below regarding SEN pupils). Form time should be as it was in the old days (yes, I know I sound like a government minister!); a time for teachers/form tutors to catch up with pupils and to catch up with each other. To have casual conversations about what is happening. To laugh, to discuss concerns. These are important to mental well-being. Allocate time to just 'be'. Ask staff to use these times to interact with pupils and build relationships. To give pupils time to raise concerns. To discuss any upcoming school events that may be causing concern. Talking is important. Relationships are important.

N.B. Silent reading is an awful activity for SEN pupils. Give other options as well, or provide technology to help them read.

Support staff are important

AKA Is your first aider a friendly person?

Support staff have a large role to play in helping pupils belong. They should be included in emotional literacy training and supported to develop listening skills. I know of great support staff who regularly receive disclosures because they aren't intimidating, and pupils trust them. They've built positive relationships.

Also, think about your first aider(s). It's important they have understanding and sympathy. They may well be dealing with self-harm issues and must never say things like "Well, that's silly, what does a pretty girl like you want to do that for?" They must also have some understanding that pupils may present with an illness that is psychosomatic. First aiders need training and understanding of mental health issues, how to listen and validate.

Chapter summary

- Belonging affects academic performance.
- Ensure the first experience of your setting is a positive one.
- Transition periods are very important to mental health and well-being.
- Ensure all pupils have a voice and are listened to.
- Work to make PE a positive experience.
- There is limited evidence reward systems are effective and they need to be monitored.
- Provide mental health training for support staff.
- Allow time for relationships to build.
- Provide a 'safe place' for vulnerable pupils.

Pupil transition – ideas and suggestions:

BEFORE THE FIRST DAY:

Transition passports

- Design a passport to be completed by the pupil.
- The passport allows the pupil to tell their new school all about themselves.
- Ask which two or three friends they would like to be grouped with.
- Include questions about their transition concerns.
- Try not to make the passport word-heavy.
- Allow for artistic flair in their answers.

New-setting booklets

- Written by current pupils in new setting.
- Gives information current pupils feel is important for new pupils.
- Again, ensure it's not too word-heavy.
- Consider producing in digital media format, like a video.
- Don't be afraid to talk about difficult issues, such as what to do if you are being bullied.
- Describe what extracurricular clubs are available.
- Talk about special days such as sports days/competition days.
- Share 'unwritten' rules of the school, like which areas tend to be for older pupils during breaktimes.

Previous school visits

- Send key transition staff to visit pupils in their current setting.
- Conduct assemblies with the pupils transitioning.
- Spend time with the new pupils in their current class.
- Allow questions from pupils when in their class.
- Ask previous schools to let you know any concerns the pupils are talking about.
- Discuss with the pupils about:

o induction day procedure
o the concept of having different teachers (for secondary levels)
o advice for moving around the school
o what happens at school lunches
o how to make new friends
o what to do about bullying
o main school regulations
o school uniform
o homework procedures and expectations.

INDUCTION DAY:

Give lots of information in advance

- What will happen on the day – start and finish times, break and lunch times.
- What to wear.
- What the procedure at lunchtime will be.
- What money or resources they will need to bring.
- Where to be dropped off and picked up.
- Consider structuring the timings of the day to match the previous setting.
- Put pupils into their new form groups/classes so they can familiarise themselves as soon as possible.
- Separate transition pupils from school pupils during lunchtime as this can be quite an intimidating time.
- Ask older pupils to spend the day with each class and help them get around.
  Send a follow-up questionnaire to induction day pupils so you can address any concerns.

SUMMER HOLIDAY ACTIVITIES (OR IF BREAK BEFORE NEW START):

- Suggest pupils practise getting to and from school.
- Put up a video on the school website walking around the school.
- Have a FAQ section on the school website for pupils to check during the holiday.
- Suggest ideas on how to make new friends.
- Remind pupils of what will happen on their first day.

AFTER FIRST DAY:

- Show some leeway in regulations; pupils will take time to settle in.
- Explain rather than punish breaking of school regulations.
- Monitor vulnerable periods such as break and lunchtimes to watch for pupils who may be having trouble settling in.
- Expect friendship 'issues' and help pupils learn how to resolve them.
- Ask staff to feed back on pupils who don't seem to be settling in so you can monitor and provide extra support.
- Schedule friendship 'teas' and events (cake).
- Support pupils attending clubs and activities.
- Set up buddy systems within their class.
- Involve older school pupils to mentor and support new pupils.

PUPILS WHO WILL NEED EXTRA SUPPORT:

SEN

- Liaise with SENCo at previous setting regarding their needs.
- Have an additional induction day/session before main one where everybody attends.
- Provide a SEN booklet with additional SEN information for parents and pupils.
- Make sure all necessary support is in place for induction and when they start.
- Ensure pupils know where to go if they have any problems.

EAL

- Involve the EAL coordinator in the transition team.
- Discuss tried and tested strategies for supporting learning used in previous setting (if applicable).
- Set up a procedure for contacting and communicating with parents.
- Use photographs and pictures to help familiarisation.

Single pupils

- They may be only pupil coming from their setting.
- They may have been socially isolated at their previous setting.
- Consider grouping single pupils together in one class to allow them to form their own friendship group.
- Arrange for them to meet and form friendships with each other before induction day.
- Discuss how to make friends.

Pupils who have been bullied

- Acknowledge their experience and the impact on their mental well-being.
- Explain the bullying procedure in your setting.
- Ensure they know where to get support in the new setting.
- Discuss what to do if they are being bullied.
- Ask staff to keep an eye on them and 'big them up' by praising them often.

Parents who have had bad education experiences

- Consider a home visit before induction day.
- Use pictures and photographs to help student familiarise themselves with the setting.
- Do not use acronyms or jargon when talking about school.
- Acknowledge their educational experience and discuss how it could be different in their new setting.

MAKING PE A POSITIVE EXPERIENCE FOR ALL PUPILS:

- Have a flexible PE kit to allow for different-shaped bodies.
- Give choices as to which activity/sport they participate in – team or individual.

- Involve pupils in choosing activities for the curriculum.
- Try not to make pupils wear PE kit from the lost property box if they haven't got theirs.
- If you have a PE kit for pupils who forgot their kit, make it nicely cleaned and folded in a variety of sizes so it's not a humiliating experience.
- Monitor changing times – in my experience a lot of bullying and self-esteem damage takes place whilst pupils are changing unsupervised.
- Some schools ask pupils to come in wearing their PE kit on PE days to reduce the difficulties and anxieties around changing.
- Break down instructions into smaller tasks.
- Do not give more than two instructions at once and be prepared to repeat.
- Praise the taking part and not the competitive element (competition can be saved for interhouse or interschool events).
- Do not set up a team captain who picks out pupils. Allocate pupils to a team.
- Speak to reluctant pupils in advance about their concerns and how you can help them view PE as a positive experience.
- Ensure you use body-positive language and discuss healthy eating rather than demonising certain foods or activities.
- Be aware how shouting can traumatise children – is there another way of calling for attention from the whole group such as a whistle or bell?
- Do use positive language (sports psychology) to motivate pupils.

References

1   OECD (2017). *Students' Sense of Belonging at School and Their Relations with Teachers, in PISA 2015 Results (Volume III): Students' Well-Being.* Paris: OECD Publishing. [1 May 2019]. Available from: https://doi.org/10.1787/9789264273856-11-en

2   West, P, Sweeting, H & Young, R (2010). *Transition Matters: Pupils' Experiences of the Primary – Secondary School Transition in the West of Scotland and Consequences for Well-Being and Attainment.* [Online]. England: Routledge. [1 May 2019]. Available from: www.tandfonline.com/doi/full/10.1080/02671520802308677

3   Rice, F et al (2018). *Identifying Factors That Predict Successful and Difficult Transitions to Secondary School.* [Online]. England: UCL. [1 May 2019]. Available from: www.ucl.ac.uk/pals/sites/pals/files/stars_report.pdf

4   Hyacinth, B (2017). Employees Don't Leave Companies, They Leave Managers. 27 December. *Linkedin.com.* [Online]. [3 May 2019]. Available from: www.linkedin.com/pulse/employees-dont-leave-companies-managers-brigette-hyacinth

5   Ryan, R.M & Deci, E.L (2018). *Self-Determination Theory.* New York: The Guildford Press.

Chapter 5

Positive motivation

Positive motivation is supportive of mental health

AKA Negative motivation is damaging to mental health

It's your performance management review with the big chief. They say to you:

"You're one of the worst members of staff I have ever had. You aren't good at your job and you're letting down the whole school. If you don't improve you are going to ruin your future".

How does that feel? Do you feel motivated to improve? Most of us wouldn't. A few of us would come out thinking "I'm going to show you" and work like a dog to prove them wrong. However, that's a minority and it's not a healthy motivation. I would come out feeling like pants and resenting them. Also, likely to look for another job. (Perhaps you're getting an idea of why I'm self-employed.)

Negative motivation doesn't work, yet we use it with pupils all the time. If you don't pull your socks up, you will fail your exams and your life will be ruined. You'll be letting everybody down. Then we wonder why mental health issues are on the rise and exam anxiety has increased. Negative motivation is bad for our mental health. It affects our self-esteem and leads to ruminative negative thinking. What's the point of trying? I'm rubbish and stupid. I'm not loveable because I'm not good enough.

We need to take a leaf out of the sports psychology book. (Yes, I am looking to sports as a good example, don't faint.) They understand the power of positive motivation to improve performance. To improve the belief in yourself.

Use positive motivation similar to sports psychology

AKA Usain Bolt didn't win because his coach threatened him with detention if he didn't

Sports psychology has been shown to improve the performance of high-level sports men and women. It's often said that mindset is the difference between winning and losing at the highest level. Yes, lots of hard work is involved, but positive motivation drives us to put the hard work in and improve performance. We are intrinsically motivated from positive motivation. Not because we will let everyone down or be thrown out of school if we don't win. Intrinsic motivation is far more powerful.

Ryan and Deci, in their book, *Self-Determination Theory*,[1] say:

> "We see the highest quality learning and achievement occurring when students' interest and engagement in learning are supported, rather than when educators rely on extrinsic incentives and controls to pressure students toward a narrow set of preordained outcomes".

They also show how positive intrinsic motivation is important to self-esteem and mental well-being. There is also lots of research to show that a positive outlook can help you live longer![2]

Believing negative motivation is necessary

AKA But I need to warn them what will happen if they don't try harder

Do not think of blue monkeys. *Blue monkeys*. Do not think of them. *Blue monkeys*. What are you thinking of? Yes, blue monkeys. If I hadn't mentioned blue monkeys you wouldn't have thought of it. Now you can't stop thinking about them.

If you are walking up on stage and someone says "Don't trip", what do you then immediately worry about? If they hadn't mentioned tripping, you wouldn't have thought of it. It's the same thing. Why talk about failure, why put it in their heads that they might fail? We listen to negative thoughts a lot easier than positive thoughts. Warning them won't change their motivation, it will simply put more negative thoughts in their head, increase anxiety and affect performance.

I am often asked to speak to Year 11 pupils about exam anxiety. Can I help them with strategies to manage it effectively? Sure. I run a group session and by the end everyone is feeling great and positively motivated, knowing how to manage their anxiety. Then a senior leader comes in and shouts at them because they're not working hard enough, or there are extra revision sessions planned because this is the most important stage of their life. Right. So, I may be understanding where the increased anxiety is coming from.

I recently spoke to a mindfulness practitioner who is regularly asked to 'run a little mindfulness session' just before exams to help with anxiety. Again, the belief that an intervention will 'fix' things without looking at what is contributing. Likely there will be negative motivation used before and after the mindfulness session which will then be blamed for not 'fixing' it.

Describe the behaviour you want

AKA Telling me what not to do puts that idea in my head

We are very good at describing behaviour we don't want and not saying the behaviour we do want. Even though I am an adult, if my mum says "Don't touch that", guess what I want to do? Yep, touch it! I have to do it. If my mum hadn't mentioned touching it, I wouldn't have touched it. I'm not saying it's her fault; I'm demonstrating the importance of language in behaviour. It's the same with pupils. There is a concept in behavioural science called 'nudge theory'. Positive reinforcement and subconscious directions influence our behaviour. This is how using positive and negative language works; it nudges us either way. Use positive language to describe the behaviour you do want, not the behaviour you don't want. Having worked with pupils excluded from mainstream settings, I quickly learned that saying "Don't throw that chair" wouldn't elicit the response I wanted. If I said "Thank you for putting the chair down" or "Do you mind if I sit on that chair" I would get a different result. This comes under the blue monkeys idea. Thank you for not talking, thank you for listening. It's much more positive language, more effective and more conducive to positive mental well-being. Nudge the positive way!

Labelling

AKA Pupils will live down or up to our expectations

Have you heard of the Pygmalion or the Rosenthal effect? It's where other people's expectations of a person affect that person's performance. (Not easy to say after a dentist appointment.) Rosenthal and Jacobson[3] conducted a study where all teachers in a Californian study were told they had some gifted and talented in their class. They called them "intellectual bloomers". These intellectual bloomer pupils were selected at random and the list given to the teachers. Those who were believed to be gifted by the teachers had made more gains than the other pupils at the end of the test period. Take that in. Those pupils who were expected to achieve more by teachers, did achieve more. This suggests we subconsciously treat people differently according to our expectation and prior labelling. Is this the nudge effect acting on us?

Labelling can also affect the way we see ourselves. A study by Grolnick, Ryan and Deci in 1991[4] showed that pupils with SEN had lower perceived competence and autonomous motivation than pupils who did not have SEN. There was also a famous study completed in India that showed that when pupils were made aware of each other's caste, the lower-caste pupil performed significantly worse in the activities they were asked to complete. Labelling affects our own self-belief and in turn our performance.[5]

Now I know self-belief and motivation aren't going to perform miracles. Someone could inspire me to believe I could run a marathon – it wouldn't happen. Firstly, I don't run. However, it may inspire me to take up running and work towards running the marathon. I want to do it, so I will make an effort. (N.B. This isn't a challenge to anyone to inspire me to run, it's just an example.)

It is important that we use positive motivation and don't label pupils or have reduced expectations because of a label. Also don't allow them to have lower expectations of their ability (one of the arguments against setting by ability). Try to be aware of your expectations of a pupil – are they as a result of labelling subconsciously? As a teacher we pick up pupil 'types' quickly and this affects our behaviour. You can pretty much always identify the naughty ones first (same as when conducting staff training). When there is disruption in the class you will automatically look at the expected naughty pupil as a result of preconceptions. They might not have been the disruptive one, but we could then catch them innocently talking to someone and we could then pounce. The pupils then pick up on who are the 'naughty pupils' and will change their behaviour accordingly. This means their behaviour is held more to account than non-labelled pupils. All this has a knock-on effect to pupil mental health and well-being.

We will automatically label and judge as part of being a human. I'm just asking you to be aware of it and understand the value of using positive motivation for all pupils for mental well-being and performance.

Embrace failure

AKA Failure is OK!

Part of positive motivation/resilience/self-esteem is reframing how we think about failure. Failure is part of life and it's a good thing. It is not something to be avoided or afraid of. Many, many successful people talk about how learning from their failures led to their success. In the Hindu religion one of the main gods is Shiva, the Destroyer. Shiva isn't seen as a bad god; Shiva is a revered and vital god. Shiva is the 'Transformer' – he destroys to recreate new life. We should have a similar mindset with failure. Failure is a good thing because we learn from it. It is necessary to move forward. In education we should use more positive language around failure. We should talk about our failures and what we learned from them, how they shaped who we are today.

I have learned a lot in my life from my failures. I learned not to run on to grab the red dodgem car before all the dodgem cars have come to a complete stop. I have learned I need to warn the medical staff of the inappropriate things I might say when coming round from anaesthetic. I have learned that whilst failing my Maths O Level felt like a major trauma at 15, it wouldn't have any effect on my later life. I learned that drawing the shape of a pig around a chicken's digestive system wouldn't fool the examiner in my agricultural science exam. And these points lead on to the next important thing about failure and positive motivation.

Failing teaches us important lessons for our mental health

AKA Laughing is good for your mental health

Exeter University came up with what they believe to be the three best strategies for managing stress, anxiety and difficult times:

- acceptance
- reframing
- humour

These link into failure and to positive motivation (that's why this is in this chapter). If we learn these strategies to deal with our failures, we can move forward positively, and it won't detrimentally affect our mental health. We will have learned something from it.

Acceptance – yep I failed, no what ifs or blaming things. I failed. And that's OK.

Reframing – putting a positive spin on it. I learned what to do next time or it has led to better things.

Humour – laughing about it. Laughter is great and so important to mental health. One time I was made redundant and very upset. My housemates were sympathetic but the next morning they woke me to point out they had jobs to go to and I didn't. It was funny. It helped. Laughing reduces impact (but not too soon).

If we can teach these strategies to pupils, we are supporting their mental health and well-being. If we learn these strategies ourselves, we are supporting our own mental health and well-being as well as modelling effective strategies.

Failure of exams is not the end of your life

AKA Don't send the wrong messages about exams

Just a quick note here whilst talking about positive motivation and failure is to be careful of the messages we send to pupils around exams. These are the things that pupils have told me regarding their exams:

- "I can only take GCSEs once" – no, they only count once to school tables, but that is irrelevant for you.
- "I can't retake GCEs" – yes you can.
- "It costs money to retake them" – no, there is funding available for 16–19.
- "I have to get certain grades, or I won't be able to go to the school I want" – whilst that school has a threshold, there are plenty of other options with different thresholds and you should have been told about these.
- "I won't get into the school or university if I don't achieve certain grades" – have a look at other options as an insurance policy; having aspirations/goals is good but not if they are not flexible and they are damaging your mental health and well-being.
- "I will be loved/liked less if I do not pass/achieve a certain grade" – *never ever ever* is this true and never should this message be felt by a pupil.

If you're experiencing high levels of exam anxiety in pupils, check what messages you, and parents, are consciously or subconsciously giving to pupils. Use positive motivation, not fear, to inspire. Reassure pupils that their value doesn't increase or decrease dependent upon the result. They are loved.

Using positive motivation with parents

AKA Are your parents' evenings depressing to attend?

I attended a parents' evening once when my daughter was in junior school. The teacher had a list of things my daughter couldn't do and had to work towards. After 10 minutes I asked if there was anything my daughter could do or if she was completely incompetent. "Oh no, Mrs Garner, she's one of the top in the class". Well thanks for that. I could have gone home and berated my daughter for all the things she couldn't do which wouldn't have been fair and would have damaged her self-esteem.

I discuss relationships with parents and our positive/negative influence in a later chapter, but a mention is relevant as a precursor to the exciting chapter ahead.

Positive motivation

AKA Give us some ideas then, Garner

Look at posters around the school

Do they use negative language? Do they describe what not to do or what to do? I would rather someone told me what to do than what not to do.

Have a 'failure' day or event

Ask everyone to talk about a failure they have had and what they learned from it. Make sure all staff contribute – it's good for our mental health and well-being as well!

Staff CPD

During CPD time, ask staff to work together in small groups or pairs and write down stock phrases they are always saying to pupils. Ask them how they could be rephrased to use more positive language and a more positive response. If they are doubtful ask them to try it on each other – list negative things they are often told, then rephrase them. If it makes you feel better (even if you think it's trite), it will make the pupils feel better. Feeling better means better mental health and well-being.

Chapter summary

- Using negative motivation is damaging to mental health.
- Positive motivation will achieve better results (as evidenced in sports psychology)
- Negative motivation does not inspire.
- Describe the behaviour/action you want (nudge effect/theory).
- Labelling can lead to reduced expectations.
- Embrace failure.
- Laugh.
- Be aware of subconscious messages around exams.
- Use positive language with parents.

Supporting tools and activities

BEST POSSIBLE SELF ACTIVITY (FOR YOURSELF AND PUPILS)

- Lots of research to show this one works to help intrinsic motivation. And remember, it's about you and what you want, not what you think other people want of you.[6]
- Take a few minutes and think about what your best possible life is – 6 months ahead, 1 year ahead, 5 years ahead maybe even 10 years ahead.
- Imagine things that are reachable and attainable, e.g. I wouldn't visualise being a famous footballer or supermodel.
- Now describe this best life – in words or pictures.
- Think about the character strengths and talents you have to achieve this best life.

- Think about the steps you went through to achieve this best life.
- Decide how you are going to start working towards this best life today. Write down your plans in as much detail as you can.
- Do this exercise regularly and when you are feeling demotivated.

REFRAMING FAILURE

"Failure is not falling down but refusing to get up".

Chinese proverb

- What did not work out as you expected?
- Do you know why it did not turn out as you hoped?
- Why has this disappointed you?
- What will you do differently next time or in the future?
- What have you learned from this?
- It's important we remember that we are not failures. This event does not mean you are a failure. What are the good things about you?
- What will you tell yourself about this event now and in the future?

References

1 Ryan, R.M & Deci, E.L (2018). *Self-Determination Theory*. New York: The Guildford Press (p 354).
2 Stibich, M (2018). How Positive Thinking Can Help You Live Longer. 30 June. *Verywell Mind*. [Online]. [1 May 2019]. Available from: www.verywellmind.com/positive-thinking-and-aging-2224134
3 Rosenthal, R & Jacobson, L (1992). *Pygmalion in the Classroom: Teacher Expectation and Pupils' Intellectual Development* (Newly expanded ed.). Bancyfelin, Carmarthen, Wales: Crown House Pub. ISBN 978-1904424062
4 Grolnick, W.S, Ryan, R.M & Deci, E.L (1991). *Inner Resources for School Achievement: Motivational Mediators of Children's Perceptions of Their Parents*. [Online]. USA: American Psychological Society Inc. [1 May 2019]. Available from: https://selfdeterminationtheory.org/SDT/documents/1991_GrolnickRyanDeci.pdf
5 Hoff, K & Pandey, P (2003). *Why Are Social Inequalities So Durable?* [Online]. USA: University of Pennsylvania. [1 May 2019]. Available from: www.piketty.pse.ens.fr/files/HoffPandey2003.pdf
6 Niemiec, R.M (2013). What Is Your Best Possible Self? 29th March. *Psychologytoday.com*. [Online]. [1 May 2019]. Available from: www.psychologytoday.com/gb/blog/what-matters-most/201303/what-is-your-best-possible-self

Chapter 6

Behaviour systems

Behaviour management systems impact mental health

AKA This isn't about having to put up with disruptive pupils

This book is about supporting mental health and well-being of staff and pupils; how to support and ensure we aren't damaging. This chapter is about the effect behaviour management systems have on mental health. Your behaviour management should not damage the mental health of pupils. It's difficult to use my amazing humour in this chapter because it's an area I feel so passionately about, and quite frankly we are bloody cruel to some of our pupils which isn't funny. I am not saying keep disruptive pupils in class. You don't have to keep disruptive pupils in class. What I am saying is don't compound mental health issues with the systems you have in place, in and out of class.

People must do the right thing or be punished

AKA Behaviour management can become dangerously obsessional

I previously mentioned one of the CBT "musts" we tell ourselves that cause stress and anxiety – we must be worthy to be loveable. The second must (there are three) is that people must do the right thing or be punished. However, everything is perception and our perception of what is the right thing. We have all broken a law or a rule. Some of us would have been caught and punished, some of us would have got away with it. Perhaps we didn't see the law as important (e.g. speeding), or it was a mistake e.g. going to get your hair done and forgetting to put a pay-and-display ticket in your car. And yet, when other people break a law/rule that they value, they want thunder to strike them dead from the skies and for their name to be besmirched forever! People speeding when they don't agree with the speed limit or they think they are a safe driver is OK. *but*! If someone parks over a white line in the supermarket car park they must be photographed and named and shamed on Facebook.

The key with behaviour management systems in schools is that they can become obsessional. The pupil must have that consequence regardless of the circumstances because they broke that rule. Staff become incensed if regulations are not followed but overlook if they don't follow regulations or ignore instructions from the leadership team. They can overlook that the behaviour system isn't making any improvements to behaviour at all, but insist it must be continued with because, those are the rules! (I am using a lot of exclamation marks in this chapter!)

I recently visited the bridge on the River Kwai in Thailand and rewatched the film *Bridge over the River Kwai* the same evening. The Alec Guinness character's determination to 'do the right thing the British way' became obsessional regardless of the outcome. They would build the bridge properly because that's how it must be, regardless of the damage that building the bridge would do transporting munitions to kill British soldiers. Some schools have become that way with behaviour. "This is our system. There is no evidence it works, and we may be damaging pupils, but we have to follow the system". (This isn't a verbatim quote from anyone, just my interpretation of a particular mindset.)

I recently read a thread on Twitter. The mother and a pupil were living in a domestic violence situation. The mother was struggling to leave for a variety of reasons. The school her son was at had a behaviour management system that had 'consequences' for pupils not bringing the right colour pens to lesson. The mother rang the school in the morning to say she had been hospitalised by a violent incident the previous night and her son would be distressed and need support. He then got to lesson to find he didn't have the correct colour pen. So, he was reprimanded. Already finding it difficult to manage his emotions because of the trauma from the night before, he took issue with this with the teacher and the situation escalated. He ended up in an isolation booth for the day. Because he forgot a pen. This is cruel and hugely detrimental to the mental well-being of a child. A child. Because he didn't have a pen. Are you picking up on my despair here? Do I need more exclamation marks?

N.B. I don't understand the colour pen marking systems – people usually pick red and green. Guess which are the most common colours colour-blind people struggle with? Red and green!

What is the purpose of your behaviour system?

AKA If you want to really rehabilitate and change behaviours then consider the following

I have yet to see any evidence that zero-tolerance systems and isolation punishment work. Yet some settings have strict behaviour systems, perhaps because they want to 'get rid' of children who don't fit their system. They can then claim they 'turned the school around'. Having an unrealistic strict behaviour system the pupil can't adhere to is a means to permanently exclude the unwanted pupils. Settings can go through the process and eventually permanently exclude pupils or 'transfer' them to another setting. I understand why some educators do this, as our current system rewards results. But they are overlooking the damage they do to the 'don't fit' pupils and the mental harm they are causing pupils who can't go along with the rigid system. With the 'don't fits' they use language such as "We don't have the facilities to support them" or "They need proper specialist help". False concern.

If you care about all children and want a behaviour management system to change behaviours and rehabilitate, then consider the fantastically intellectual points I raise here, and read work of other fabulous people such as Jarlath O'Brien, Paul Dix, Paul Garvey, Nina Jackson, or Ian Gilbert (to name just a few).

Every system has to have flexibility

AKA Use some common sense and compassion

Whatever your behaviour management system is, it has to be flexible. There must be flexibility to take into account mitigating factors. Even our justice system does this – charges and sentencing vary according to each circumstance. There has to be the ethos that punishments are adapted according to the situation and the pupil. It's not a one-size-fits-all. Pupils should be treated as individuals. The purpose of a behaviour system should be to support pupils managing their emotions and improving behaviour.

Isolation booths do not work and are damaging to mental health

AKA Isolation booths really do not work and really are damaging mental health

Remember, the three common elements in most mental health conditions are low self-esteem, social isolation and ruminative negative thinking. Strict, inflexible behaviour systems hit all these. Low self-esteem – unable to follow strict rules so the pupil is singled out and made to feel different and incapable. Social isolation – kept away from friends, no restorative or therapeutic conversations. Ruminative negative thinking – sat in isolation with nothing to do but 'reflect on bad choices' or repeat negative thoughts in their head all day. This is how isolation booths damage mental health, particularly for pupils who are already vulnerable and suffering.

There is a wealth of research that shows the damaging effect of solitary confinement for prisoners[1] and yet we do it to children? I have yet to see any evidence that isolation booths have a positive effect on a pupil. Yes, I understand that some pupils need to be removed because of the impact on other pupil learning, but that doesn't mean isolation. That is a poor argument.

There is also the factor that many pupils are missing a high number of lessons because of isolation. They are then expected to go back into class, know what they've missed to 'catch up', as well as improve their behaviour, as highlighted in a recent court case.[2]

Positive relationships always improve behaviour

AKA It's not about control and fear

I often run into ex-pupils where I live, always a nice experience. I remember meeting a young man who had experienced a lot of challenges at school and who was a member of the therapeutic behaviour unit I established. The first thing he said to me was "Sorry I was a t**t at school, Miss". We carried on talking about what he was doing now, school days, etc. and then he randomly asked me who I thought he was most scared of at school. I said I thought it was probably Mr Hairdryer Treatment Teacher (expelled a lot of hot air loudly). He said "No, it was you, Miss. I didn't want to let you down". That is the power of positive relationships. It's not about fear or control. It's about positive relationships.

One day (here we go) the wind and the sun were having an argument as to who was the strongest. The wind insisted he was (yes, I am making the bad character a man, but I didn't say they were a PE teacher . . .) and suggested a competition to see who would win. He pointed to a PE teacher (oh . . .) walking up the street with a coat on. "Let's see", said the wind, "who can get that PE teacher's coat off the quickest". "OK", said the sun. The wind went first and started to blow the PE teacher. But the man just buttoned his coat up. The harder the wind blew, the tighter the man drew his coat around him. Eventually the wind blew out of puff and gave up. So, it was the sun's turn (you know where this is going). She shined on the PE teacher and as he got warmer and warmer, he took his coat off. Ta-da! A sickly sweet analogy but so true. Positivity is always more effective and more supportive of mental health.

One study showed that suspensions were halved when staff were trained in a more empathetic approach. Is that not the aim of behaviour systems – to improve behaviour and reduce the need for exclusions/punishments?[3]

Punitive measures alone do not work

AKA Look at the evidence to support positive behaviour change

Some people in education have the mentality that "children only misbehave because I haven't found the consequence severe enough to stop them". Prisons are full of people that show this mentality doesn't work. Punitive measures alone do not work, or even punitive measures do not work. In their book,[4] Ryan and Deci discuss at length and evidence how excessive control, reward and punishment systems do not lead to positive behaviour change, often the reverse. They show how education staff who supported pupil autonomy and self-regulation, along with boosting pupil self-esteem, had higher levels of learning and fewer behavioural problems. This highlights that if your behaviour system relies on punitive measures alone, it is less likely to change behaviour and more likely to damage mental health. This also affirms so much I've previously said about positive relationships and self-esteem, etc.

Pick the right staff to support positive behaviour

AKA Don't do the usual strong male in charge using fear as a tool

Look at who is in charge of your behaviour system. Very often it's male staff. Often 'strong' male staff. We believe that these staff are the most effective but that's not always the case. Remember I talked way back about how violent teenagers turned around their behaviour in part by developing relationships with adults who modelled self-regulation. If your 'strong male' can show self-regulation and build relationships without shouting, great. If you have a member of staff who uses shouting and fear as a regular tool, this is not effective and is damaging to mental health. My ex-pupil was most 'scared' of me, not the shouty male teacher. He didn't want to let me down because we built a positive relationship. By the way, he had a great job and was engaged to a lovely girl. Also, as stated previously, shouting can affect already traumatised children and increase their feelings of anxiety and threat.

Pick staff who are able to model self-regulation. Staff who have good emotional literacy, and an understanding of why children behave as they do. Staff who can have constructive conversations discussing more positive behaviours. This isn't 'do-gooder' staff who want to be their 'friends', as I recently heard. It's about modelling self-regulation and effecting positive change. We don't learn from being told what not to do or by being punished for doing the wrong thing. Remember the (brilliant) positive motivation chapter.

Consider how strict your behaviour system is

AKA Don't set up unnecessary confrontations

I don't understand the need to have overly strict behaviour systems or zero tolerance. Why do we expect developing pupils to adhere to set standards we are not able to adhere to as adults? There is a belief that we have to have ultimate control, and control means respect. Except it doesn't. It's setting up unnecessary confrontations that are completely irrelevant to learning and damaging of mental health. If you pick at me constantly for the little things, that will damage my self-esteem. It will also hinder the building of positive relationships which are so important to learning, and life.

School uniform – it isn't a leveller. It doesn't command respect and it doesn't improve learning.[5] We are one of the few countries in the world obsessed with uniform. Do we have less crime as a result? Better behaved adults? Statistics don't support that. If you do have a uniform, why isolate someone from learning because they don't have polishable shoes? I really don't understand the logic in that. Have you been to Google and hi-tech company offices? They wear jeans and what they want, as do most of us as adults. There are some careers with strict uniform rules, e.g. the forces, but they make the choice to sign up to the regulations, and they get paid for it.

There are also issues around self-esteem linked to uniform. If you have a strict uniform policy deciding exactly what people must wear in and out of the classroom then you are likely damaging self-esteem. We are all different body shapes and physically develop at different levels. Physical differences are a big deal for pupils. To not allow a pupil to wear a jumper or blazer in class when they may be plus size, have self-harm scars, or be very self-conscious of a particular body part is damaging to self-esteem and mental health. At your next staff meeting insist all staff take their jumpers/coats/jackets off. They won't want to and will feel vulnerable if they do. It's the same for pupils.

Clothes make us feel safe. We choose clothes that make us feel comfortable. It's important to our mental health. When low, I will be in pyjamas and a hoodie. Hoodies are amazing pieces of clothing to hide in and feel safe. We have to give pupils the opportunity to cover areas of their body they are concerned about. There was a study looking a youth suicides over the period of 2014–2015.[6] They found that 33% of pupils who died by suicide during that period had a physical health condition, the most common being acne or asthma. It suggests that their physical condition had drastically affected their self-esteem. We also need to allow adolescent pupils to wear some make-up to help their self-esteem and to cover areas they feel vulnerable about. Never, ever, ever, as a punishment for wearing make-up, take out make-up wipes from your drawer and ask the pupil to remove make-up there and then in front of everyone (I know this happens). That is an awful thing to do – total humiliation and incredibly damaging of self-esteem.

Coloured pen system

I previously mentioned a system where pupils have to bring in certain colour pens, and if they don't then that triggers stage 1 in the behaviour management system. Why not just have a box of pens at the front of the room? Brains don't mature until mid-to-late 20s and have lots of changes taking place. Many SEN pupils will struggle with organisation all their life. Why punish over something so trivial? It's an unnecessary confrontation. It doesn't affect learning and it doesn't indicate that they are not worthy of teaching. Some of the most brilliant people I know are always forgetting things and losing pens – including teachers! Again, why do we expect children to achieve a higher standard than we do as adults?

Is your behaviour management system discriminative?

AKA Strict behaviour management systems are discriminative

Look at the demographics of pupils being punished as part of your behaviour system. More often than not it is not reflective of the demographics of the school and certain categories of pupils will appear highly. Why is that important to mental health? Because the 'regularly punished pupils' are likely to be vulnerable pupils that are more likely to suffer from a mental health condition. SEN pupils, for example, are six times more likely to suffer from a mental health issue and they are most likely to feature in exclusions/punishment statistics. In 2016–2017, SEN pupils accounted for approximately half of permanent and fixed-term exclusions in England.[7]

This is discrimination. It's not as obvious as punishing a wheelchair pupil for being late to class as the lift didn't work, which is why many people don't make the connection. Discrimination affects mental health. If your system is discriminatory you need to change it.[8,9]

Fresh start each day

AKA Don't carry punishments over the weekend or holidays

If you have a system whereby a pupil 'owes' a certain number of days in detention, don't carry these over weekends or school holidays. Ideally each day should be a fresh start. By 'carrying over' punishments you are ensuring that your setting is not a safe place for pupils. Imagine a vulnerable pupil with a chaotic home life. He/she doesn't feel safe at home. School should be their safe place, but they struggle there. They come in at the beginning of a new term or week feeling relieved to be away from home, perhaps optimistic they are going to try harder that week. They arrive and are placed in the behaviour unit for the day. How does that make the pupil feel? Why would they come into school? How is it improving behaviour and learning? Imagine you are walking through the door of work on a Monday and the first thing that happens is you are berated by SLT for something that happened last term and sent to a cupboard on your own all day. Do you feel motivated to change your behaviour for the good?

The use of language when 'managing behaviour'

AKA I hate the term *behaviour management*

The language we use is important to our mental health. Constant use of negative language is damaging to our mental health, as I have discussed in previous chapters. The term 'behaviour management' is a negative term. It suggests that behaviour is something to be managed rather than supported or changed. It's confrontational already. I haven't yet thought of a snappy positive term to replace behaviour management. 'Supporting pupils to make positive changes' doesn't quite have the right ring. I've heard the term 'low-arousal environments' as well, but it's not catchy. If you think of something let me know!

We must consider the language we use around behaviour and its effect on the mental health of the pupil. Negative language reduces the likelihood of changing the behaviour of the pupil. When we tell pupils they made a "bad choice" or they "behaved that way on purpose", this is negative. Remember, all behaviour is communication.

When children do not grow up in nurturing environments and/or experience trauma, their body produces toxic chemicals. These toxic chemicals in childhood reduce the size of the amygdala and hippocampus. The amygdala and hippocampus are responsible for processing emotion, memory and managing stress. A smaller amygdala and hippocampus mean children are less able to manage stress, have a reduced ability to react appropriately and experience a greater level of fear and anxiety. They are more likely to 'overreact'. Building positive relationships, modelling self-regulation and metacognition are key factors in changing this.[10]

Using language such as 'choice' around behaviour isn't accurate or helpful. Being told that you are choosing to behave in such a way, when it is a reflex action or learned behaviour, is damaging to self-esteem and mental health. I've worked with children who believed they were evil. Just nasty people that deserved to be punished. Think about the language you use. I've made some suggestions, based on CBT, at the end of this chapter as suitable positive conversations that will be more effective in achieving positive change.

Be aware of our automatic response when threatened

AKA Pupils laughing when being reprimanded is an automatic response as well

Everyone knows about Fight, Flight or Freeze – Our natural reactions when we are feeling threatened or extremely panicked. There are actually two more: Flop and Friend. Flop is when a person goes into a completely dissociative state and everything shuts down, usually after Freeze hasn't worked. I mentioned my big horse-riding accident. I can remember coming off the horse and being on the ground but nothing in between. I had shut down to manage the pain and trauma of lots of bones snapping (added for dramatic effect there). The other reflex is Friend,[11] where we try to 'friend' the threat by laughing or smiling and thus, disarming them. We want them to see we are nice person and be our friend. So, if a pupil laughs when they are being reprimanded, it isn't disrespectful. It's a reflex action and they may be in a state of panic, so you might reduce the threat.

So, what should we do?

AKA Marvellous ideas to think about

Use time out of the classroom to effect positive change – when outside of the classroom, use the time effectively. Have therapeutic conversations, talk about why they did what they did or what they could have done differently. Role play situations to practise a different response. Discuss what other options were available. There is a CBT activity at the end of this chapter that can be used as a conversation template.

Set realistic targets – poor behaviour will not suddenly change. Targets for behaviour improvements have to be realistic and small steps. Allow each small step to become habit before moving on to the next step. This is how therapeutic behaviour change happens. "Your target this week is to wait 10 minutes before calling the teacher a t**t instead of five minutes".

Have a flexible behaviour system – the criminal justice system has a guide for punishments, but it is a range, as there are mitigating factors to be considered. We all understand this, and school behaviour systems should do the same. There should be guidelines and thresholds, but flexibility to take other factors into account.

Consider mental health issues in your uniform policy – have a flexible uniform policy that encompasses pupils of all shapes and sizes. Consider mental health issues such as eating disorders, self-harm, etc.

Chapter summary

- Behaviour management systems can negatively affect mental health.
- Implementation of punishments can become obsessional.
- Systems have to be flexible.
- Isolation is damaging to mental health.
- Positive relationships achieve far more.
- Pick the right staff to support behaviour change.
- Do not have overly strict rules to set up confrontation.
- Ensure your system is not discriminating against groups of pupils.
- Have fresh starts every day.
- Use positive language around behaviour.

Supporting tools and activities

CBT Conversations to Effect Behaviour Change

What happened?

How did it make you feel?

Why do you think it made you feel like that?

What did you want to happen?

Did you get the result you wanted?

Do you think that was the best outcome/result?

What other options did you have?

Would those options have had a better result?

What can you change about how you react next time this happens?

What can you tell yourself when you're getting angry?

Consider a self-esteem exercise/conversation after this or as part of the process

CBT conversations to effect behaviour change – Example worksheet

What happened?

> *Mr T shouted at me to sit down so I swore at him and walked out*

How did it make you feel?

> *Angry and stupid*

Why do you think it made you feel like that?

> *Because I hadn't done anything wrong*

What did you want to happen?

> *I wanted to get thrown out of class*

Did you get the result you wanted?

> *Well, yes but I walked*

Do you think that was the best outcome/result?

> *Yes, cus I didn't speak to him but no cus I missed my lesson*

What other options did you have?

> *Ask him not to shout. Sit down*

Would those options have had a better result?

> *Sitting down would have*

What can you change about how you react next time this happens?

> *Just sit down and not get angry*

What can you tell yourself when you're getting angry?

> *It doesn't mean I am stupid. I can control my behaviour*

Consider a self-esteem exercise/conversation after this or as part of the process

Behaviour change plan

What is my behaviour target?

What are the steps to me achieving my target?

When will I attempt the first/next step?

What do I need to tell myself when taking the first step?

Who will help me with the first step?

How did the first step go??

Behaviour change plan – Example worksheet

What is my behaviour target?

To stay in all of my lessons

What are the steps to me achieving my target?

*Stay calm when teacher shouts at me. Not get distracted by others
Not to swear if I don't stay calm. Talk to Mrs G if I'm struggling*

When will I attempt the first/next step?

My next lesson with Mr T

What do I need to tell myself when taking the first step?

I like myself, I am calm and everything will be okay

Who will help me with the first step?

Mrs G and the learning support people

How did the first step go??

It went okay. I didn't walk or get kicked out

References

1 Coid, J et al (2003). *Psychiatric Morbidity in Prisoners and Solitary Cellular Confinement, I: Disciplinary Segregation*. England: Routledge. *The Journal of Forensic Psychiatry & Psychology*. 14, 2: 319 (p 298). doi: 10.1080/1478994031000095510

2 Perraudin, F (2018). Court Challenge to Use of Isolation Booths for Disruptive Pupils. 1 March. *The Guardian*. [Online]. [2 May 2019]. Available from: www.theguardian.com/education/2018/dec/11/pupil-brings-legal-action-against-schools-isolation-booths-outwood-grange-academies-trust

3 Okonofua, J.A, Paunesku, D & Walton, G.M (2016). *Brief Intervention to Encourage Empathic Discipline Cuts Suspension Rates in Half Among Adolescents*. [Online]. USA: PNAS. [2 May 2019]. Available from: www.pnas.org/content/113/19/5221.abstract

4 Ryan, R.M & Deci, E.L (2018). *Self-Determination Theory*. New York: The Guildford Press.

5 Educationendowmentfoundation.org.uk (2019). Educationendowmentfoundation.org.uk – toolkit. [Online]. [3 May 2019]. Available from: https://educationendowmentfoundation.org.uk/evidence-summaries/teaching-learning-toolkit/school-uniform/

6 Appleby, L et al (2017). *Suicide by Children and Young People National Confidential Inquiry into Suicide and Homicide by People with Mental Illness (NCISH)*. [Online]. England: University of Manchester. [2 May 2019]. Available from: http://documents.manchester.ac.uk/display.aspx?DocID=37566

7 Department for education (2018). Permanent and Fixed Period Exclusions in England: 2016 to 2017. 19 July. DfE Exclusion Statistics. [Online]. [3 May 2019]. Available from: https://assets.publishing.service.gov.uk/government/uploads/system/uploads/attachment_data/file/726741/text_exc1617.pdf

8 Emerson, E, & Hatton, C (2007). The Mental Health of Children and Adolescents with Learning Disabilities in Britain. *The British Journal of Psychiatry*. 191: 493–9.

9 Mcintyre, N (2018). *Thousands of Children with Special Needs Excluded from Schools*. 23 October. *The Guardian*. [Online]. [2 May 2019]. Available from: www.theguardian.com/education/2018/oct/23/send-special-educational-needs-children-excluded-from-schools

10 Sunderland, M (2006). *What Every Parent Needs to Know*. England: Dorling Kindersley. 2007, 2nd ed.

11 Lodrick, Z (2010). Psychological Trauma – What Every Trauma Worker Should Know. 20 November. *Zoelodrick.co.uk*. [Online]. [3 May 2019]. Available from: www.zoelodrick.co.uk/training/article-1

Chapter 7

Working with parents

Working with parents

AKA Building good relationships with parents has better outcomes for everyone

Why do we have a chapter titled "Working with parents" in a mental health book? There are three key reasons. Firstly, because there is a vast array of research showing that good home-school relationships improve achievement, and improved achievement supports good self-esteem. Secondly, our relationship with parents can have a knock-on effect to the pupil (I will explain later). Thirdly, this book is also here to support the mental health of staff (the first chapter and very important). Positive relationships with parents will reduce stress levels for staff.

How does it affect the pupil?

AKA I can back this up with research

Many studies show that positive parent-school relationships improve outcomes for pupils, including academic and prosocial outcomes.[1] The prosocial element we have already seen is very important to mental health. It's also common sense: if we all get along life is easier.

Legacies from the past

AKA Acknowledging the poor school experience many parents had

For most of us who work in education, school wasn't a bad experience. We must have quite liked it – otherwise we wouldn't have chosen to go back and work in that environment.

(Of course, it may have traumatised us now.) But this isn't the case for everybody. We have to acknowledge that for many people and parents, school was a traumatic experience. They hated it and these memories still affect their opinion of schooling today. Parental cognitive bias transmits to their children.[2]

Thinking about my pupil days, when I attended a rural comprehensive school, we had 'remedial' classes who were told they wouldn't achieve much – they would be more vocational. All the school attention went to those who were academic and there were distinct social groups. There was also bullying of pupils by teachers and humiliation was regularly used as a 'motivation'. I am left-handed but I was still made to slant my 'joined-up' writing the way right-handed people do. I also remember passing pupils standing outside the headmaster's door waiting for the cane. Using physical violence seems so awful now, although some emotionally illiterate people still advocate the use of violence!

The knock-on effect of a bad school experience for parents is twofold. Firstly, school will be an intimidating place for them. They won't want to attend, and it will bring back the feelings of uselessness and failure. It's like running to into an ex who ditched you and you're wearing no make-up, with greasy hair and trampy clothes. But worse, they know they're going to have to go back.

Secondly, they will want to protect their child from the same experience. As a result, they will likely be very defensive and sometimes aggressive, to protect their child from having the same experience. We will all defend our children from any event that we perceive as traumatic, and for some parents that is school and teachers.

We cannot expect all parents to have a positive outlook of education. We have to acknowledge this. No, it wasn't you as you weren't in education at the time, but remember how important validation is, way back in the first chapter. We must validate parents who had a poor school experience. We have to show it's different now. That it's changed. "I'm really sorry you had such a bad school experience. I hope to show you it's changed now and how we can work together to help Johnny have a more positive experience and achieve".

Respecting the parent

AKA Don't judge or look down on parents

Every setting should have an ethos of respecting all parents. All of them. They genuinely love their child more than you do. They may struggle to show that, or have not been shown positive parenting techniques, but they should still be respected. We are all products of our past and some of us were luckier than others. And it is luck. I didn't show any skill by being born into a 'good' family. It's luck of the draw. Some parents were born into families with trauma, poverty, dysfunction, etc. Doesn't mean they are less worthy of our respect. Potentially they deserve more respect because they are surviving each day in situations I would struggle with.

The key is, every parent is doing the best they can. Indeed, I believe everyone is doing the best they can. At any moment, we are all doing the best we can at that time. Yes, I could be better at housework but that's not a priority for me so I'm not putting my all into it. The same with parents. For some parents getting through the week on the limited money they have is their priority, not making cakes for a bring-and-buy sale or helping with homework. We have to understand that parent priorities may be different to ours, and their practical parenting skills are based on their experiences. No one is a crap parent on purpose.

Understanding parental pressures

AKA It's bloody hard for a lot of parents

I discussed earlier how we currently have a society that rates good parenting as having children who achieve academically. As a result, parents will put pressure on their children to achieve academically to make them feel they are good parents. They will feel they have succeeded (or failed) as a parent. This pressure isn't good for mental health or well-being of pupils – there is a difference between motivation and excess pressure. We have a duty to help change this narrative and reduce pressure on parents for the mental health and well-being of all of us. We must not perpetuate the myth that a high-academic-achieving child is the sole measure of good parenting. Academic achievement is one measure but not the only measure. Good mental health and well-being is more important.

The number of working parents is higher than when I attended school.[3] Getting time off to attend school events is hard. Time at home together is limited and having to help your child make an exact replica of Pompeii with papier mâché and Fairy Liquid bottle adds more stress. We have to acknowledge and understand the wide range of pressures on parents, to ensure we don't add to the pressures. Parenting is bloody hard.

As part of our respect for parents and understanding parental pressures, it's also important we are careful sending out edicts to parents. I've seen them on social media, condescending letters about looking up from mobile phones and not to wear pyjamas to drop your child at school. If someone put a notice up asking parents to not wear pyjamas to drop their child at school, I would purposefully wear pyjamas to all school events. Do not judge me. Do not act superior. This will not build a good relationship.

Don't add to parental pressures

AKA Book Day is fine but leave it at that please

Following on from the Pompeii replica I mentioned previously, often schools have many activities and days that involve a lot of extra work for parents and it becomes competitive. When my children were in school, we enjoyed Book Day each year but then it got stupid. We had Evacuee Day, Spanish Day, Viking Day, etc. Then 'take the teddy bear home and take photos' weekends. Come on! As a parent it's another stick to beat yourself with for being crap. There are always parents who will go over top with costumes. "Oh, I messaged friends in Sweden to send over a traditional Viking costume" as you're stood there holding a baseball cap with two pipe cleaners sticking out. Please don't have loads of these days. Do they really enhance learning or just reinforce social groupings and compound which pupils are poor? Many parents struggle financially, and time-wise, and then feel guilty which isn't good for their mental health and well-being, or their child's. That's not the purpose of education. Yes, I knew my pipe-cleaner-hat children were more resilient than the children with the authentic costume (and they were ginger, so that was Celtic Day sorted), but that didn't stop me feeling like a crap parent and resenting the school for arranging that day's 'events'.

Then there's the 'the take the school bear home for weekend' exercise. Take pictures and write a story. With some parents the bear comes back with a story of visiting Buckingham Palace and sitting in the throne whilst chatting with David Beckham. When my children had the bear, we had "Oh here's the bear next to Mummy exhausted snoring on the sofa", "Here's the bear sat in the trolley in Asda whilst Mummy is shopping" and so on.

Fortunately, my mum is an expert at sewing so with enough notice my children didn't miss out. However, lots of children did, through no deliberate fault of the parent, which damages home-school relationships. I also resented feeling pressured to compete. If it was just me, I would have taken a stand and sent my children in in normal uniform. However, I didn't feel my seven-year-old and nine-year-old would understand the importance of 'fighting the system' and I hated the thought of them 'standing out'.

So please. Don't have too many 'character' days and provide costumes for children whose parents have a lot of pressures in their life, financial- and time-wise.

Our influence on parent-pupil relationships

AKA We have more influence than we think

We know that stress isn't good for mental health and being a parent is stressful. We must try not to add unnecessarily to parent stress as it can have a knock-on effect for the pupil. Think about times you have been highly stressed; when something unexpected happens you are more likely to snap at someone (as discussed in Chapter 1). If you're a stressed parent and you keep getting negative phone calls from school, or you come back from a parents' evening disappointed because of the language used by the teacher, who are you going to snap at? The pupil. I know, because I've done it. Then felt guilty. And it's not helpful to the mental health and well-being of the parent or pupil.

Parents are mostly impressed by teachers. Teachers are generally seen as clever academic people (except PE teachers obviously). As a result, they will take the word of a teacher. If a teacher tells a parent their child is lazy and doesn't work hard enough, the parent will believe that and berate them. That will be more people not understanding all behaviour is communication and using negative motivation to change the behaviour. Behaviour is unlikely to change, and the pupil's self-esteem will be damaged. The language we use is important.

No, you/we aren't responsible for how a parent treats their child, but we can have a positive effect. Building positive relationships with parents reduces stress and improves mental well-being for all of us (as already mentioned). Don't underestimate the influence you have and the knock-on effects of what you say.

Positive motivation also works with parents

AKA Threatening rarely achieves a positive outcome

I've been to lots of meetings where pupils had behavioural or attendance issues. The seriousness of the meetings would escalate up to higher levels of SLT and more intimidating meeting rooms. The final meeting was in the boardroom with the headteacher and SLT. We sat on opposite sides of the room and the parent was told their child would be permanently excluded if the behaviour/attendance of their child did not improve. Not once in those meetings have I ever heard a parent say "Well, I haven't been parenting to the best of my ability and I have got other strategies I haven't used. Now I know how serious it is I will make more effort, so they improve". Using intimidation, environmental and verbal, doesn't work. Parents are doing the best they can. What we need to do is work together to help improve the situation. Try to find out the difficulties and how we can effect positive change.

Think of these situations from the parents' point of view. You didn't like school and you know you are being called into a high-level meeting likely to throw your child out. You're put in an intimidating room with lots of staff on the other side from you. You are told all these things that are wrong with your child and how their life outcomes are poor. You've tried all you know, and home life isn't easy because of money/single parenting/housing/full-time work but here you are being threatened and you've had enough. You will likely become aggressive and/or give up.

Now think of a different meeting. You're called into school. You know your child has been struggling. You're invited into a meeting without tables, no 'them and us' seating, and you're offered a cup of tea. You're told that your child has many fabulous qualities and they are listed, but they are struggling in some areas and school would like to work together to help your child. Is there anything they can help with or do you have any suggestions?

Which meeting is going to inspire you to work together to effect positive change?

It's the same as discussed in the behaviour chapter. If you want to simply go through the formalities so you can exclude the child, use the threatening way. If you really want to effect changes and improve outcomes for all, use the positive motivation method and language.

It starts from the beginning

AKA How welcoming is your school

We talked about how welcoming your setting is to pupils in an earlier chapter. It's the same for parents. First impressions count. Is the signage to reception clear and easy to read? Is it easy to get in the door? If you have to press a button for reception, is it clear where the button is and what you should do? I've stood a lot of times outside a school like a lemon trying to work out how to get in. When you get in is the reception welcoming? Are your receptionists friendly? Do you have to wait for them to finish their conversation about last night's TV and open a small glass window you have to bend down to before you can speak? Do they say "Hello it's nice to see you, can I get you a drink?" No, your setting isn't a hotel, but these things make a big difference to everyone, all visitors. If you have a parental meeting arranged, the tone of the meeting will be set by the initial welcome. What sort of meeting outcome do you want? Positive or negative?

Contact parents for positive reasons

AKA Don't keep ringing and moaning about their child

You know how you have friends who only ever contact you when they want to moan, or they have something negative to say. Parent-setting relationships can be like this. I remember a conversation with a parent whose children were struggling with school regulations. He hadn't been answering his phone, so I visited the house. He wasn't particularly pleased to see me (a rare occurrence obviously) and when I asked why he wasn't answering the phone or answering my messages he said "Why would I, you only ever ring to moan at me about my children". And he's right. In the same way you avoid calls from the negative friend, parents avoid calls from school. They do get to the stage of "Just exclude them and send them home".

I know some schools have a policy of reporting two positives to one negative to parents, on school reports, report cards, etc. I just call this a shit sandwich. Imagine I see you in the street and I say "Wow, love your handbag and dress [I am superficial], but your hair is a mess – what happened?" Are you going to walk away thinking "Oh, she loves my dress and bag"? No, you're going to walk away thinking "*My hair is a mess, nightmare!*" When you eat a shit sandwich you don't remember the nice bread, you remember the pooh. Not that I've tried of course.

We've discussed the use of positive language and the importance of working together. Try to contact parents just for nice things and that's all. Just because. Not "They're doing really well, but . . . "

Actively engage parents

AKA An open-door policy isn't enough

Many schools tell me they have an "open-door policy" with parents. That they are always welcome. However, there are many parents that don't use this, or attend parents' evenings or events. We think that a 60% turnout for a parents' evening is good and pat ourselves on the back. But is 60% good enough? It's likely that the 40% not attending are parents of pupils who need more support. Again, at the end of this chapter I make suggestions as to activities to improve parent engagement and attendance.

Consult with all parents

AKA Don't just ask the opinions of parents who make nice cakes or who will say nice things

Do you conduct parent surveys about them, not just about the pupils? Do your parents have a voice? Again, parent voice is important and contributes to the well-being of your pupils. I know many schools consult parents, but how many schools work to consult *all* parents and ask questions about the parents, not just the pupil? We need to ask the opinion of all parents to find out how we can build positive relationships and break down barriers. There are suggested questions to ask at the end of this chapter.

Parents with specific needs

AKA They need support too

School is part of the community and will sometimes have to provide extra support for parents. Many schools do this successfully and become community hubs. Their staff and pupils benefit as a result. I've heard of many schools providing fantastic support such as:

- food banks
- second hand uniform shop
- adult literacy and numeracy classes
- EAL parent social groups
- housing and benefit advice
- parenting support groups

Amazing initiatives. Reducing stress on families for the benefit of the pupil. There will be parents who have literacy difficulties or whose first language isn't English. There are also parents with SEN – remember 10% of the population has dyslexia, so that includes your parents. What does your setting do to support parents and families? We are part of communities and have a role to play.

So what should we do?

AKA Marvellous ideas to improve parent-school relationships

Use less formalised language

Parents are more likely to attend informal events, so use less formal language. I would attend anything called "Cake Night". Pupil Recognition Night, Celebration Evening, that sort of thing. Positive language will lead to improved attendance.

Specifically invite parents

If you specifically ring and invite parents who do not usually attend, they are more likely to attend. Part of CBT is that the more detail you plan something in the more likely it is to happen. So, when working with a client about a new activity they are going to try, you plan it in as much detail as possible and discuss possible eventualities. It's the same with parents. Contact them, ask them to come, discuss times, do they have transport, etc. Also, explain what will happen when they arrive at school, thus reducing the anxiety of attending. Tell them you are looking forward to seeing them!

Contact parents who couldn't/didn't attend events

Contact parents who didn't turn up to events and ask them what you can do to support their attendance next time. If parents know you noticed they weren't there and they were missed, they are more likely to make an effort next time.

Make parents' evenings positive events

Make them nice to attend. Ensure they will hear positive things about their child and 'areas for development' rather than weaknesses or failures. Talk about targets.

Event welcome

At any parent event provide a 'welcomer' or two – someone who smiles and says hello, who direct parents where to go, explains what will happen, etc. This makes a difference and parents are more likely to attend other events. We always seem to manage the welcome at open days for prospective new pupils –let's carry this on. Do not put an intimidating teacher at the entrance with folded arms, who rocks back and forth like a prison guard (it's been done).

Reduce jargon

Use language normal people will understand. Starting a meeting with "Well, Mrs Jones, Sarah is two levels below where she should be according to our Fisher Family Trust predictions and in class she is not using key vocabulary identified by her teacher. She is not attentive during the plenary part of her lesson and often makes no record of the follow-up tasks she has to complete". Right. Thanks then. Use normal language. If you use acronyms, explain what they are. Perhaps produce a 'jargon-buster' explanation sheet. Positive working partnerships are the key, not intimidation.

Explain how to help with homework

Many parents do not help with homework because they feel they have to have subject knowledge. This isn't the case. Discuss with parents how they can support their child's homework without subject knowledge. For example, providing a quiet place to complete the homework, listening to their child discuss what they have to do, etc.

Make parents' evening appointment systems simple and easy

Basically, leaving it up to the child to book appointments will mean that likely, those children who don't really need the support of parents' evening will be the ones making appointments. Design a simplified system that is accessible by all – perhaps allow parents to use an online appointment system or ring in to make appointments. Maybe staff call parents to make appointments. Yes, I know time is difficult, but remember the Upstream/Downstream parable. By building positive relationships we are getting upstream, which will require less time downstream for all.

Report positive achievements and events

We discussed this in the self-esteem chapter. Making positive remarks about pupils will improve relationships with parents. I like people who like my children. If you don't like my children, or act like you don't like my children, we are not going to have a positive relationship. Remember to avoid the shit sandwich.

Use a variety of communication methods

Use social media – it is being successfully done by many schools. Also use vlogs on your school website to talk about latest news. Letters are OK as long as you don't use lengthy language. Keep it succinct and easy to read. Remember to avoid education jargon.

Chapter summary

- Building positive relationships with parents has good outcomes for everyone.
- School-parent relationship can impact pupil mental health and well-being.
- Many parents will have had a negative school experience.
- We have to respect all parents.
- Parents are under a wide range of pressures.
- Don't have too many school 'days'/events.
- We can negatively and positively affect parent child relationships.
- Use positive language with parents to achieve better outcomes.
- Ensure your school is welcoming.
- Actively engage and invite parents.
- Consult with all parents.
- Support parents with specific needs.

Supporting tools and activities

PARENTAL SURVEY SUGGESTED QUESTIONS

N.B. These are additional to the usual 'Is your child happy at school' surveys.

- Do you feel welcome at our setting?
- If not, how could we make you feel more welcome?
- Are school letters and school reports easily understand and free of educational jargon?
- What are the barriers for you attending school for events/parents' evening?
- How could we help reduce those barriers to enable you to attend?
- Do you have any specific needs you would like us to be aware of, e.g. dyslexia, English as a second language, physical disabilities?
- Do you have any suggestions as to how we could improve our relationships with parents?
- Would you like advice on how to support your child in school?

Consider:

- Is the survey accessible to all?
- Is it available in all applicable languages?
- Could you conduct home visits/telephone surveys for some parents?

References

1   Jeynes, W.H (2007). The Relationship Between Parental Involvement and Urban Secondary School Student Academic Achievement: A Meta-Analysis. *Urban Education*. 42, 1: 82–110. https://doi.org/10.1177/0042085906293818

2   Remmerswaal, D, Muris, P & Huijding, J (2016). *Transmission of Cognitive Bias and Fear from Parents to Children: An Experimental Study*. England: Journal of Clinical Child and Adolescent Psychology.

3   Chapman, B (2017). Number of Working Mothers with Dependent Children in UK Surges by 12 Million. 26 September. *The Independent*. [Online]. [2 May 2019]. Available from: www.independent.co.uk/news/business/news/working-mothers-with-dependent-children-uk-surges-1-million-office-for-national-statistics-a7968486.html

Chapter 8

From the top down

Mental health and well-being is not an add-on

AKA It must be embraced by all

For any setting to truly have a positive effect on the mental health and well-being of its staff and pupils, it has to include the SLT. It has to be embedded in the ethos of the setting and embraced by all.

I facilitate a lot of training on mental health and I often hear "I've been sent on this training so I can deal with pupil mental health". As the training progresses it's clear that the management has no intention of changing any of their practices or looking at their role in mental health and well-being throughout the setting. Instead they are paying for them to go on a course to fix it. The management are looking for a few interventions that they can implement to sort the problems. It doesn't work that way. Part of supporting mental health and well-being is ensuring that your systems aren't harming pupils. I know the whole academic system isn't always helpful in our desire to support all pupils; however, there is a lot we can do within our settings, as outlined in this book.

Different approaches to mental health and well-being

AKA Which one is your setting?

Having travelled nationally and internationally to many settings, speaking to many people and experiencing many systems, I have come across some approaches to whole setting mental health and well-being that are less successful than others. Here are some of them:

1 There is no problem

The setting doesn't have a mental health problem. It's just snowflake nonsense and they just need to have a stiff upper lip.

2 The peacock approach

The setting likes to make a big show of all their fabulous interventions but behind all that it's basically arse. They have all these interventions to say how marvellous they are, but they won't actually look at what they are doing to contribute. They should not be expected to make changes themselves; "We've been doing marvellously for years and there are no problems (that we acknowledge)".

3 Can you come in and fix it but . . .

These settings invite specialists in to speak to staff and/or pupils about mental health, maybe during a well-being day, once a year. No SLT attend and as soon as the event has finished, the setting and processes carry on as they always did and nothing really changes. The specialist has fixed the teacher/pupil, so all is good.

4 The pat-on-the-back approach

These settings believe they support mental health and do it very well. They know they support it well because they discuss it as an SLT and discuss all the fabulous things they do to support it. "That's great! Do you ask the staff or pupils?" No, but they don't need to; they know already.

5 They are interested as long as you say the right thing

Yes, they survey their staff and pupils on mental well-being and how they feel it is supported in school. They insist on their names, though, and will challenge staff if they say something bad. They also don't release the results of the survey if it makes them look bad.

Your setting may be one or many of these. Or your setting may be a fabulous setting where SLT get it, understand and are making positive changes in the life of staff, pupils and parents. I have met some amazing senior leaders who 'get it' and they are really making a positive difference in the lives of their staff and pupils. The approach of the SLT to mental health and well-being as a whole in the school is really the first foundation brick.

It starts with SLT as individuals

AKA SLT members must be emotionally literate and have good understanding

When I am discussing mental health and well-being, the reception often depends on the emotional literacy and self-awareness of the person I am talking to. Part of changing mindsets about mental well-being is about changing our own first. Whenever I learn something new or undertake a new course, I always apply what I have learned to myself. If I have a 'growth mindset', I can understand more about myself and I can try to understand more about others. It also helps me develop my unconditional positive regard (UPR), which is a fancy term for not judging others, and recognising we are all doing the best we can at that time.

A reaction of many people when I talk about mental health is to think about applying it to others. "Ah yes," they say, "I can see that is a problem for Jo Bloggs, so how do I tell them what they're doing wrong, so they can change? Or, how could I use what you've said to tell my daughter/husband/friend where they are going wrong and that's the problem in their life?" That's not how it works. The only person you can change is you, and what you do. By changing that, we affect change in others. By supporting others, we can be positive influences on their life. Remember we don't fix, and people don't need fixing.

SLT members have to be open to improving their emotional literacy and understanding, open to knowing all the scientific background of brain development and trauma and open to knowing why all behaviour is communication. They must know why staff mental health and well-being is a priority (the very first chapter) and they must look at the systems in place in the setting and how they manage staff to ensure that they, as individuals and as a leadership team, are not having negative and detrimental effects on the positive mental health and well-being of staff and pupils.

Individuals do make a difference

AKA You can still make a positive difference even if your SLT isn't on board

If you're reading this and you're not on the SLT, or you are but the rest of the SLT isn't ready to embrace the concepts in this book, don't worry. You can make a difference individually to the lives of pupils. A massive difference. There are so many things you can take from this book and implement yourself, lots of research on how one person can make a difference. Remember:

- Children who are empathised with on a regular basis in childhood have a good vagal tone (calm body states), and do better academically, socially and emotionally.[1]
- When people talk about their feelings, rather than pretending all is OK, their body and mind are calmer and more regulated.[2]
- When people are in pain, an empathetic presence calms the body.[3]
- "Teachers are well placed to act as the significant, caring adult in a young person's life".[4]
- "Considering serious barriers precluding youth from accessing necessary mental health care, the present meta-analysis suggests child psychiatrists and other mental health professionals are wise to recognize the important role that school personnel, who are naturally in children's lives, can play in decreasing child mental health problems."[5]

If you are an individual 'fighting the fire' in an unsympathetic setting, make sure you don't try to do it all yourself. You will burn yourself out. Do what you can whilst looking after yourself. It will make a difference.

Look after yourself

AKA You can't work effectively if you neglect your mental health and well-being

This applies to all of you reading this, whether you are part of the SLT or not. Your well-being has to take priority, echoing what we said in Chapter 1. Don't burn yourself out in the process of trying to support pupils. You are much more effective if you can be positively selfish and take regular time for yourself to boost yourself up. You can't pour from an empty cup, etc. Also, working with people who don't 'get it' with regard to mental health and well-being can be incredibly frustrating with regard to the emotional pain you see in pupils (one of the reasons I am self-employed; I have a low tolerance of ignorant people). Do what you can, it does make a difference, and look after yourself first.

Remember

AKA If you only take away a few things from this book, make it this

Three common factors to mental health issues:

- low self-esteem
- social isolation
- ruminative negative thinking

Three elements of happiness:

- relatedness/belonging
- autonomy
- mastery/competence

You don't have to be an expert. Make sure you are a good role model, and that you listen, hear and acknowledge.

Make sure you are supporting mental health and well-being and not damaging.

Thank you.

References

1 Gladstone, G.L, Parker, G.B & Malhi, G.S (2006). *The Journal of Nervous and Mental Disease* (Volume 4, Issue 3 pp 201–8 ed.). New York: Wolters Kluwer.
2 Lieberman, M.D et al (2011). *Subjective Responses to Emotional Stimuli During Labeling, Reappraisal, and Distraction*. CA: UCLA.
3 Sambo, C, Howard, M, Kopelman, M, Williams, S & Fotopoulou, A (2010). Knowing You Care: Effects of Perceived Empathy and Attachment Style on Pain Perception. *Pain*. 151: 687–93. doi: 10.1016/j.pain.2010.08.035
4 Howard, S & Johnson, B (2000). *Resilient and Non-Resilient Behaviour in Adolescents*. Trends & issues in crime and criminal justice No. 183. Canberra: Australian Institute of Criminology. Available from: https://aic.gov.au/publications/tandi/tandi183
5 Sanchez, A.L (2017). *The Effectiveness of School-Based Mental Health Services for Elementary-Aged Children: A Meta-Analysis*. [Online]. USA: Florida International University. [2 May 2019]. Available from: www.jaacap.org/article/S0890-8567(17)31926-3/fulltext

Chapter 9

Checklist

If you want to look at implementing some of the amazing ideas from this book, here is a checklist that may be useful for you.

Chapter 1 – Staff

- Staff regularly receive mental health awareness training including how the brain develops and the impact of Adverse Childhood Experiences.
- Staff know how to support a student in distress – listen, hear and acknowledge.
- Staff are positive role models of self-regulation.
- Staff are able to discuss their mental well-being openly without fear of reprisals.
- All staff are encouraged to maintain a positive work-life balance.
- The setting is a fun place to be and laughter is encouraged.
- Staff are appreciated and regularly reminded of their value.
- The staffroom is a nice place to be.
- Activities and procedures are in place to actively support staff mental health and well-being.
- There is a definite support system for staff who need mental health and well-being support.
- Staff are regularly surveyed regarding their mental health and the mental health and well-being of pupils.

Chapter 2 – Self-esteem

- The importance of positive self-esteem is understood by all staff.
- All pupils are valued equally – academic pupils are not rated more highly.
- Friendship groups are supported in school.
- Socially isolated pupils are identified and supported in making friends.
- Staff model positive empathetic responses inside and outside the classroom.
- Pupils are provided with a range of opportunities to display talents, not just academic.
- The setting has looked at research regarding setting by ability and considered alternatives.
- Achievements outside of school are recognised and valued.

Chapter 3 – Bullying

- The setting acknowledges bullying takes place.
- The effects of bullying on pupil mental health and well-being is understood.
- The setting has a strong definition of 'bullying' that staff and pupils are all are aware of.
- The terms 'target' and 'perpetrator' are used.
- The bullying policy is regularly reviewed.
- Staff and pupils are consulted, anonymously, on the effectiveness of the policy and procedures.
- Pupils can report bullying anonymously.
- The setting takes preventative measure to help pupils who are more likely to be bullied – e.g. self-esteem work, building friendships.
- The setting is respectful of all and does not operate a hierarchical system based on academic achievement.
- Staff are mindful of not abusing their power over pupils.
- Perpetrators are provided with therapeutic support to increase understanding of their behaviours.
- Restorative-justice-type solutions are not implemented without the approval of the target.
- Targets are supported to manage possible future bullying incidents.
- Targets are provided with therapeutic support to counteract the possible effects on their mental health and well-being.
- Perpetrators are not shouted at as a punitive measure.
- Supervised areas for vulnerable pupils are provided during unstructured times.

Chapter 4 – Pupil experience

- The setting provides a welcoming first experience for pupils.
- We have a rigorous transition process that considers the mental health and well-being of all pupils.
- Any school council is demographically representative of all pupils.
- School council is consulted on a wide range of issues.
- Pupils are able to provide feedback outside of the school council.
- The importance of PE for mental health is understood and valued.
- The PE curriculum is flexible to suit the needs of individual pupils.
- PE lessons are a welcoming and enjoyable experience for all pupils.
- The setting has a safe haven for pupils to 'run' to.
- Form time is a relaxed time for pupils and tutors to 'catch up' and discuss any concerns.
- Support staff have received training in supporting pupil mental well-being.

Chapter 5 – Positive motivation

- The power of positive motivation is understood and embraced as a concept.
- Negative motivation is avoided.
- Staff describe the behaviour they want.
- Staff are aware of the detrimental effect of labelling and try to be conscious of any negative cognitive bias.
- Failure, and what was learned from it, is regularly discussed.

- Negative messages about the importance of exams are avoided.
- Parents are regularly told positive messages about their child.
- Posters and regulations around the school use positive language to describe the desired behaviour.
- Staff model laughing at mistakes.

Chapter 6 – Behaviour systems

- The behaviour system is flexible to take mitigating factors into account.
- The behaviour system actively supports positive behaviour change and isn't purely punitive.
- Isolation booths or time in isolation are not used.
- We work hard to build positive modelling relationships with 'challenging' students.
- Supportive staff who model self-regulation manage our behaviour systems.
- Regulations are not unnecessarily strict to set up confrontation.
- School uniform takes account of the many differing needs of students.
- Behaviour system data is regularly monitored to ensure discrimination against pupil groups is not taking place.

Chapter 7 – Working with parents

- The setting h0as a commitment to build positive relationships with parents.
- Staff understand some parents may have negative perceptions of education.
- All parents are respected.
- The setting does consider the pressures on parents when arranging events or 'character' days.
- Staff recognise how their language to parents can negatively impact pupils.
- Parents are regularly told of the positives of their child in school.
- The setting is welcoming to all parents.
- Parents who don't attend events are contacted to ask how they can be supported to attend in future.
- Parental surveys regularly take place.
- Additional parental needs, such as SEN and EAL, are considered and taken into account.
- Educational jargon is avoided in communications.

Chapter 8 – From the top down

- SLT understand the importance of their involvement in supporting mental health and well-being.
- SLT regularly undertake training to support their mental health and well-being, to develop their emotional literacy, and understand how their setting can have a positive or negative impact on pupil mental health and well-being.
- Staff understand the difference they can make as individuals.
- All adults understand the importance of supporting their mental health and well-being first.